PENGUIN BOOKS

WORLD WAR ONE

'A gem' Harry Mount, *Spectator*

'A brief, easily digested narrative of the First World War that
is studded with epigrams . . . Stone offers what few British
historians can: the view from elsewhere, a sense of what the
war looked like outside the Western Front'
Robert Hanks, *Independent*

'Cogent and pungent . . . he has a marvellous eye for detail'
Piers Brendon, *Guardian*

'An exceptionally gifted scholar with an enviable command
of languages, an originality of mind and an unconventional
approach that illuminates everything he has written'
Michael Howard, *Sunday Times*

'Such a readable and stimulating history'
BBC History Magazine

'Stimulating . . . highly readable' *Daily Express*

'Perfectly pitched and fact-packed' *Sunday Herald*

ABOUT THE AUTHOR

Norman Stone lives in Oxford and Istanbul. He is the author of *The Eastern Front, 1914–1917* (winner of the Wolfson Prize), *Hitler* and *Europe Transformed*. He has taught at the universities of Cambridge, Oxford and Bilkent, where he is now Director of the Turkish-Russian Centre.

NORMAN STONE

World War One
A Short History

PENGUIN BOOKS

PENGUIN BOOKS

Published by the Penguin Group
Penguin Books Ltd, 80 Strand, London WC2R ORL, England
Penguin Group (USA) Inc., 375 Hudson Street, New York, New York 10014, USA
Penguin Group (Canada), 90 Eglinton Avenue East, Suite 700, Toronto, Ontario, Canada M4P 2Y3
(a division of Pearson Penguin Canada Inc.)
Penguin Ireland, 25 St Stephen's Green, Dublin 2, Ireland
(a division of Penguin Books Ltd)
Penguin Group (Australia), 250 Camberwell Road, Camberwell, Victoria 3124, Australia
(a division of Pearson Australia Group Pty Ltd)
Penguin Books India Pvt Ltd, 11 Community Centre, Panchsheel Park, New Delhi – 110 017, India
Penguin Group (NZ), 67 Apollo Drive, Rosedale, North Shore 0632, New Zealand
(a division of Pearson New Zealand Ltd)
Penguin Books (South Africa) (Pty) Ltd, 24 Sturdee Avenue, Rosebank, Johannesburg 2196, South Africa

Penguin Books Ltd, Registered Offices: 80 Strand, London WC2R ORL, England

www.penguin.com

First published by Allen Lane 2007
Published in Penguin Books 2008
006

Copyright © Norman Stone, 2007
All rights reserved

The moral right of the author has been asserted

Typeset by Rowland Phototypesetting Ltd, Bury St Edmunds, Suffolk
Printed in England by Clays Ltd, St Ives plc

978-0-141-03156-9

www.greenpenguin.co.uk

ALWAYS LEARNING   **PEARSON**

Contents

List of Illustrations   vii
List of Maps   ix
Introduction   xi

One: Outbreak   3
Two: 1914   33
Three: 1915   63
Four: 1916   91
Five: 1917   115
Six: 1918   155
Seven: Aftermath   183

Some Sources   205
Index   215

List of Illustrations

Photographic acknowledgements are given in parentheses

Outbreak
Archduke Franz Ferdinand and Duchess Sophie   2–3
lying in state (Hulton-Deutsch Collection/Corbis)

1914
Calling up of Turkish troops in Constantinople   32–3
(Bettmann/Corbis)

1915
French 220 cannon on the Western Front   62–3
(Hulton-Deutsch Collection/Corbis)

1916
British gasmasked machine-gun unit on the Somme   90–91
(Hulton-Deutsch Collection/Corbis)

1917
Russian troops in eastern Galicia running past a   115–16
church during unidentified battle (Bettmann/Corbis)

1918
British Mark IV tank (Corbis)   154–5

Aftermath
Returning German army marching through Berlin   182–3
(Stapleton Collection/Corbis)

List of Maps

1. Europe in 1914   192–3
2. The Western Front, 1914   194–5
3. The Eastern Front, 1914–1918   196
4. The Balkans and the Straits   197
5. The Western Front, 1915–1917   198–9
6. The Italian Front, 1915–1918   200–201
7. The Western Front, 1918   202–3

Introduction

In 1900, the West, or, more accurately, the North-West, appeared to have all the trumps, to have discovered some end-of-history formula. It produced one technological marvel after another, and the generation of the 1850s – which accounted for most of the generals of the First World War – experienced the greatest 'quantum leap' in all history, starting out with horses and carts and ending, around 1900, with telephones, aircraft, motor-cars. Other civilizations had reached a dead end, and much of the world had been taken over by empires of the West. China, the most ancient of all, was disintegrating, and in British India, the Viceroy, Lord Curzon, not a stupid man, was proclaiming in 1904 that the British should govern as if they were going to be there 'for ever'.

The title of a famous German book is *War of Illusions*, and the imperial illusion was only one of them. Within ten years much of the British empire was turning into millions of acres of bankrupt real estate, partly ungovernable and partly not worth governing. Thirty years on, and both India and Palestine were abandoned.

The governments that went to war all made out that they were acting for national defence. But it was empire that they had in mind. In 1914, the last of the great non-European empires was disintegrating – Ottoman Turkey, which, in (very theoretical) theory, stretched from Morocco on the Atlantic coast of Africa through Egypt and Arabia to the Caucasus. Even then, oil had become important: the British Navy was going over to it, as against coal, in 1912. The Balkans mattered because they were quite literally in the way, on the road to Constantinople (as even the Ottomans called it at the time: *Konstantiniye*). As it happens, I have written this book partly in a room with a view over the entire Bosphorus, through which a huge volume of traffic, from oil-tankers to trawlers, flows every day and night. It is the windpipe of Eurasia, as it was in 1914.

It is ironic that the only long-lasting creation of the post-war peace treaties, Ireland perhaps excepted, has been modern Turkey. In 1919, the Powers tried to partition her, partly using local allies, such as the Greeks or the Armenians. In a considerable epic, to the surprise of many, the Turks fought back and in 1923 re-established their independence. The process of modernization – 'westernization', it has to be called – has not been straightforward, but it has been remarkable just the same. Chance – a conference on the Balkans – brought me there in 1995, and I stayed. I should like to acknowledge the support that I have had from Professor Ali Dogramaci, Rector of Bilkent University. It has been the first private university in what might be called 'the European space', and the success of its example is shown in the widespread imitation that has followed. I have encountered a great deal of kindness in Turkey, and can easily see what old von der Goltz Pasha, the senior German officer involved in the First World War, was driving at when he wrote, of his two-decade-long experiences, that 'I have found a new horizon, and every day I learn something new.' Through Professor Dogramaci, an expression of collective gratitude.

Some friends and colleagues deserve separate mention just the same. Professors Ali Karaosmanoglu and Duygu Sezer were very helpful from the first day, and I should also like to acknowledge the help I have had especially from Ayse Artun, Hasan Ali Karasar, Sean McMeekin, Sergey Podbolotov in matters Turco-Russian, and Evgenia and Hasan Ünal, who introduced me to the history of the Levant. Rupert Stone, my target reader, read the manuscript and made suitable comments, as did David Stevenson. My assistants, Cagri Kaya and Baran Turkmen, also a target readership, have kept the administrative show on the road, learned their Russian, and taught me how to manage writing machines.

In this edition, certain errors have been corrected, and I am grateful to correspondents who have pointed them out.

A NOTE ON PROPER NAMES

Author and reader alike have more important concerns, in the First World War, than strict consistency over place names that have frequently changed. I have tended to use the historic ones, where they are not fossils: 'Caporetto' makes more sense than the modern (Slovene) 'Kobarid', whereas 'Constantinople' is now obsolete. I have generally shortened 'Austria-Hungary' to 'Austria'. It is impossible to get these things right; may convenience rule.

World War One

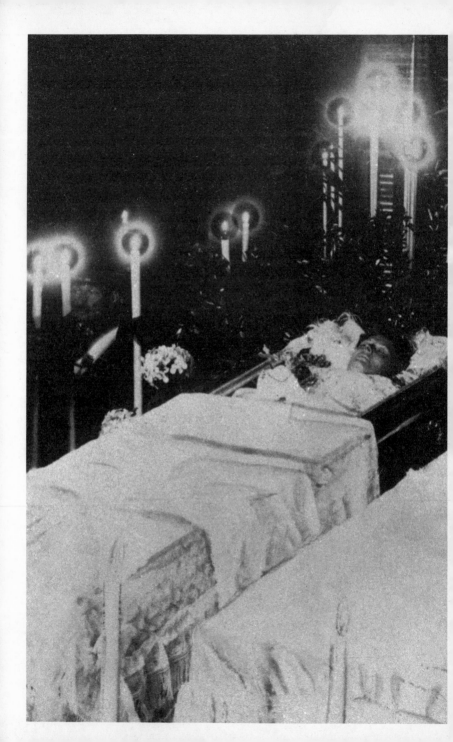

WWI

preceding pages: Archduke Franz Ferdinand and Duchess Sophie lying in state

The first diplomatic treaty ever to be filmed was signed in the White Russian city of Brest-Litovsk in the early hours of 9 February 1918. The negotiations leading up to it had been surreal. On the one side, in the hall of a grand house that had once been a Russian officers' club, sat the representatives of Germany and her allies – Prince Leopold of Bavaria, son-in-law of the Austrian emperor, in field marshal's uniform, Central European aristocrats, leaning back patronizingly in black ties, a Turkish Pasha, a Bulgarian colonel. On the other were representatives of a new state, soon to be called the Russian Socialist Federation of Soviet Republics – some Jewish intellectuals, but various others, including a Madame Bitsenko who had recently been released from a Siberian prison where she had been put for assassinating a governor-general, a 'delegate of the peasantry' who had been picked up from the street in the Russian capital at the last minute as useful furniture (he, understandably, drank), and various Russians of the old order, an admiral and some staff officers, who had been brought along because they knew about the technicalities of ending a war and evacuating a front line (one was an expert in black humour, and kept a diary). There they are, all striking poses for the cameras. It was peace at last. The First World War had been proceeding for nearly four years, causing millions of casualties and destroying a European civilization that had, before war broke out in 1914, been the proudest creation of the world. The war had destroyed Tsarist Russia; the Bolsheviks had staged their revolutionary take-over in November 1917; they had promised peace; and now at Brest-Litovsk they got it – at German dictation.

The terms of the treaty of Brest-Litovsk were quite clever. The Germans did not take much territory. What they did was to say that the peoples of western Russia and the Caucasus were now free to declare independence. The result was borders strikingly similar to those of today. The Baltic states (including Finland) came into shadowy existence, and so did the Caucasus states. The greatest such case, stretching from Central Europe almost to the Volga, was the Ukraine, with a population of 40 million and three quarters of the coal and iron of the Russian empire, and it was with her representatives (graduate students in shapeless suits, plus an opportunistic banker or two, who did not speak Ukrainian and who, as Flaubert remarked of the type, would have paid to be bought) that the Germans signed the filmed treaty on 9 February (the treaty with the Bolsheviks followed, on 3 March). With the Ukraine, Russia is a USA; without, she is a Canada – mostly snow. These various Brest-Litovsk states would re-emerge when the Soviet Union collapsed. In 1918, they were German satellites – a Duke of Urach becoming 'Grand Prince Mindaugas II' of Lithuania, a Prince of Hesse being groomed for Finland. Nowadays, Germany has the most important role in them all, but there is a vast difference: back then, she was aiming at a world empire, but now, in alliance with the West, she offers no such aims – quite the contrary: the difficulty is to get her to take her part confidently in world affairs. The common language is now English, and not the German that, in 1918, everyone had to speak as a matter of course. Modern Europe is Brest-Litovsk with a human face, though it took a Second World War and an Anglo-American occupation of Germany for us to get there.

There is much to be said for a German Europe. She had emerged as the strongest Power in 1871, when, under Chancellor Bismarck, she had defeated France, and she had gone far ahead. In 1914, Berlin was the Athens of the world, a place where you went to learn anything important – physics, philosophy, music, engineering (the terms 'hertz', 'roentgen', 'mach', 'diesel' all commemorate that era, and the discoveries on which the modern world is built). Three of the members of the British cabinet that went to war in 1914 had studied at German universities – the Secretary of State for War had translated Schopenhauer – and so too had many of the Russian-Jewish Bolsheviks whom the Germans encountered at and after Brest-Litovsk. There was no end to the ingenuity of German chemists and engineers, and the Central Powers came close to victory on the mountainous ways of the Italian front because Ferdinand Porsche invented the four-wheel drive to deal with them (and then went on to the Volkswagen and much else).[1] In 1914 the great smokestacks of the Ruhr or industrial Saxony predominated, as once those of Britain and Manchester had done. Certainly, as Churchill acknowledged, Germany produced a spectacular war effort, with victories such as the battle of Caporetto against the Italians in 1917, or the March offensive of 1918 against the British, displays of panache of which the plodders on the Allied side were utterly incapable.

The idea of a German Europe also made sense on the ground, and, again, there is a ghostly resemblance to the present. A European economic space, protected from British or American competition, including the ore of Sweden and France, the coal and steel industries of Germany, and with outrunners into North Africa and even Baghdad, where oil had already become important: why not? In 1915 one of the most enlightened Germans, Friedrich Naumann, wrote a bestseller called *Mitteleuropa* in which he called, not so much for a German empire, as for a sort of Germanic commonwealth, Berlin showing the way for the various smaller peoples to the south-east, of whom there were many. These peoples – Poles the largest group – had been swallowed up in the historic empires of Austria, Russia, Turkey; there were millions of Poles in Germany. Nationalist movements arose among most of them, and threatened the very existence of Austria and Turkey. Overall, seen from Berlin, these non-German peoples were being allowed to get away with too much. The Austrians spent so much money in a futile effort to buy off the nationalists that there was not enough left for the sinews of power – the army especially, which had a smaller budget than the British army, one tenth its size. If Austria were properly managed, with a dose of Prussian efficiency, such problems would go away. In a Germanic *Mitteleuropa*, ran the thinking, these lesser peoples, whose culture anyway owed much to Germany, would come to heel. Since 1879 there had been an Austro-German alliance. Naumann meant to give it economic teeth. Other Germans had in mind a more forceful approach.

The confidence of these Germans grew as the country's industry boomed, and success went to their heads. Bismarck had been cautious: he could see that a strong Germany, in the centre, might unite her neighbours against her. But a new generation was coming up, and it was full of itself. The symbolic figure at its head was a new young emperor, Kaiser Wilhelm II, who came to the throne in 1888. His model was England. She was vastly rich and had an enormous overseas empire. England was conservative as regards institutions, which had long historical roots, but she was also go-ahead, and her industries accounted for a large part of the world's trade. Her overall position was guaranteed by an enormous navy. Why should not Germany acquire an overseas empire to match? Under Wilhelm II, German power and the blundering expression of it became a – the – European problem.

Already, on the Continent, there was rivalry with

France, the outcome in the short term of Bismarck's great victory of 1871, when the new Germany had annexed the eastern provinces of Alsace and Lorraine, and in the longer term of a history that went back to the seventeenth century, when France had dominated Europe and perpetuated the division of Germany into quarrelling states and statelets. To Franco-German rivalry was added a further relationship of tension. Bismarck had been careful not to estrange Russia, and there was a close understanding between Berlin and St Petersburg, in part because of monarchical solidarity in general and in part because each had taken its share of a Poland that was not easily digestible. But a new factor came up in the later nineteenth century, as the Turkish empire in Europe weakened. Austria, Germany's ally, had powerful interests in the Balkans, and so too did Russia: there were Austro-Russian clashes, and Bismarck's balancing act became strained. Frustrated in their search for German support, the Russians looked to France, which anyway had money to spare for investments abroad, whereas German money stayed at home.[2] By 1894, France and Russia were formally in alliance. Matters then became much more complicated when Germany bid for world power and constructed a great navy.

In 1900 the non-European world appeared to be disintegrating. India and Africa had passed into European control; China and Turkey looked increasingly likely to collapse, and Germans wished for their share. They then proceeded in quite the wrong way, and the generation that emerged into maturity around 1890 has much to answer for. The last thing that Germany needed was a problem with Great Britain, and the greatest mistake of the twentieth century was made when Germany built a navy designed to attack her. That cause somehow united what was best in Germany. Max Weber is one of the most respected sociologists, and his gifts were enormous: languages, law, history, philosophy, even the statistics of Polish peasants buying up Prussian land. In 1895 he gave a well-publicized inaugural lecture when he was appointed to a chair at Freiburg University. He was remarkably young for such a position – not much more than thirty. The professor (who had resigned from the Pan-German League on the grounds that it was not nationalist enough) talked what now appears to be gibberish, making less sense than Hitler: England has no social problems because she is rich; she is rich because of empire; she exports undesirables – Irish, proletarians, etc. – because she has assorted Australias where they can be dumped; from these she can get cheap raw materials and a captured market; so she has cheap food, and there is no unemployment; England has her empire because she has a great navy. Germany also has undesirables – Poles, proletarians, etc. – therefore she too must dump the undesirables in colonies; a navy is therefore a good idea; England would accept a German imperial role if in a battle the German navy were large enough to do serious damage to the British navy before being itself sunk; that would mean that, come the next British naval battle, the British would not have enough ships and would therefore be sunk, by French or Russians. This was received with rapture by the audience. It is one of the stupidest documents ever put together by a clever man, and hardly worth even parodying. Every step in the argument was wrong, beginning with the assumption that the British had few social problems: these might even have been rather less without the sheer costs of empire. At the end of European imperialism, in the 1970s, the poorest country in the continent was Portugal, which ran a huge African empire, and the richest were Sweden, which abandoned its only colony – in the Caribbean – long before, and Switzerland, which never had an empire at all.

Weber had a moral sense,[3] and when he saw his young students being mown down in 1914 he refused to join the crew of professors cheering on the national cause. But he and his like had led the younger generation down a deadly path. Germany produced a navy, and it took one third of the defence budget. The money, diverted from the army, made it unable to take on the two-front war that the Franco-Russian alliance portended. There was not enough to take in more than half of the young men who could have been trained: they could not be fed and clothed. They were exempted, and the German land army in 1914 was hardly larger than the French, although in 1914 the French population stood at under 40 million, to the Germans' 65 million. The German battleships themselves were very well built, but there were too few of them, and they were hopelessly vulnerable. They spent almost the entire First World War in harbour, until, at the end, threatened with pointless sacrifice, the crews mutinied, bringing down the German empire itself. But the navy, designed only to sail across the North Sea and therefore not needing the weight of coal that worldwide British warships required, could lay on extra armour. This was such an obvious piece of blackmail that it pushed the British into a considerable effort – not only did they outbuild the Germans, almost two-to-one, in ships, but they also made defensive arrangements with France and Russia. These involved colonial bargains – Egypt for Morocco with the French (the *Entente Cordiale*) in 1904, and Persia with the Russians in 1907. There were informal understandings regarding naval cooperation if it came to trouble. To each of these steps, the German reaction was blundering and blustering – a demand for some slice of derelict Morocco in 1905, encouragement of frivolous Austrian aggressiveness in the Balkans in 1909 and a gunboat sent to Morocco in 1911. This 'sabre-rattling' went down well with a great part of opinion at home, but it created an air of international crisis, and by 1914 an emissary of the American President was talking of militarism gone mad.

Around this time there emerged a matter with which the world has had to live ever since. President Eisenhower, in the 1960s, found the right phrase for it: 'the military-industrial complex'. War industry became the most powerful element in the economy, employing thousands if not millions, taking a large part of the budget, and stimulating all sorts of industries on the side, including the writing of columns in newspapers. Besides, war industry was subject to bewildering change: what appeared to be an insane waste of money at one stage might turn out to be essential (aircraft being the obvious case), whereas what appeared to be common sense turned out to consist of white elephants (fortresses being, again, the obvious case). Technology was becoming expensive and unpredictable, and by 1911 there was an arms race. By then, any country's armaments had become an excuse for any other country's armaments to increase, and there were crises in the Mediterranean and the Balkans to make every country feel vulnerable. When Germany sent her gunboat to Morocco in the summer of 1911, she uncocked a gun. But the finger on the trigger was, peculiarly, Italy's.

If Turkish territory was to be parcelled out, then why should not Italy take her share? The British had taken Egypt, the French, North Africa. Italian empire-builders looked at the rest, and went to war. It is a strange fact of modern European history that Italy, weakest of the Powers, brings the problems to a head: no Cavour, no Bismarck; no Mussolini, no Hitler.[4] Now, Italy opened the series of events leading to war in 1914. Knowing that, because of the Moroccan crisis, the British, French and Germans would do nothing to stop her, she attacked Ottoman Turkey and tried to seize Libya. The Turks were too weak, and in any event had no ships to defend even the islands off the Anatolian coast, which the Italians seized. The prospect of an Ottoman collapse caused the various Balkan states, in the first instance, to declare their interests. In alliance, in 1912, they attacked, winning in a few weeks, clearing the Ottoman army from the Balkans. Then, in a second Balkan war (1913) they fell apart among themselves, and fought again. The Turks staged a recovery, but the victors were Serbia, which cooperated closely with Russia, and Greece, which cooperated closely with Great Britain.

When China had been disintegrating, ten years before, the Powers had also been rivals, but the rivalry was naval. If the Ottoman empire was disintegrating – and almost no one now expected it to last – then the rivalry would be nearer home and would involve land connections and armies. For Russia, the straits between the Black Sea and the Sea of Marmara or the Dardanelles between the Marmara and the Aegean were vital: the windpipe of the Russian economy. Ninety per cent of grain exports went through, and much else came in, to keep going the industries of southern Russia. During the Italian war, in 1911–12, the Turks had closed the Dardanelles; there had been an immediate economic stoppage in southern Russia. To get security at the Straits was a vital matter for Russia, and early in 1914 the Entente Powers forced the Turks to grant a status close to autonomy to the partly Armenian provinces of eastern Anatolia. This (and the parallel Anglo-French interest in the Arab provinces) might easily have spelled the end of the Ottoman empire, as the Christian Armenians might become Russian instruments. Before the treaty could be ratified, the Turks opened a line to Berlin.

Germany was the Power that threatened them least – quite the contrary, the Kaiser paraded himself as protector of Islam and gave the Sultan a vast, Germanic railway station on the Asian shore of Istanbul as a sign of approval and support. At the end of 1913 a German general, Liman von Sanders (son of a converted Jew, and therefore considered in wooden Berlin thinking to be suitable for the Orient), became in effect commander of an Ottoman army corps, placed at the Straits between the Black Sea and the Aegean. The Russians reacted against this, but they could not stop the sending of a German military mission to Turkey – several dozen specialist officers – and in any case the chief figure in the new regime at Istanbul was very clearly the Germans' man: Enver Pasha, who spoke German almost perfectly and had the kind of military energy that the Germans admired. He and other 'Young Turks' generally came from the Balkans and had learned at first hand how 'nation-building' was carried on there – a new language, militarism, expulsion of minorities. Germany was the magnet for them, whereas France or England were the models for their political opponents. For the moment, given the despair that followed upon the Balkan Wars, it was Enver and his friends who were in the ascendant, and they invited Liman von Sanders. A Russian nightmare was a Germany in charge of the Straits, and the arrival of that German military mission at Sirkeci station in December 1913 marked the beginning of the countdown to war, eight months later.

Russia might dread German control of the Straits. But there was also a German dream of empire – or, more correctly, a Central European dream, because Austria-

Hungary had also long sought commercial and political influence in the Near East, and Austro-Hungarian trade was not far behind Germany's. One of the great international wrangles of the era had concerned a German-sponsored railway, linking Berlin and Baghdad – the Kaiser's gift of a station was part of this – and by 1914 a new German embassy had been built in Istanbul (known as 'the bird cage' from the ostentatious eagles on the roof), glowering down over the Bosphorus at the Dolmabahce Palace, where skulked the resentful puppet Sultan, whom Enver and the Young Turks treated as furniture. Hitherto, Russo-German rivalry had been somewhat indirect, to do with tepid German support for Austria-Hungary. Now there was a direct clash, over Russia's most vital interest.

This coincided with heightened tension of a more general sort. The arms race had been speeding up after 1911: a new dimension in the air, a 'super-Dreadnought', more soldiers being conscripted, more strategic railways being built. Turkey was on Europe's frontier, and if there were diplomatic crises, armies – Austrian, German, Russian – were affected. Before 1914, there was a great boom in trade, and governments had money to spend. A modest German increase in army spending (to train more men) in 1911 provoked a French response (again, more men in the peacetime army) in 1912, which provoked in turn another German (and Austrian) increase. In 1913 came the decisive one: a 'great programme' that was intended to turn Russia into a 'super-power'. That programme would have given Russia more guns than Germany and, at last, would have allowed the Russian army to feed and clothe and transport more than the hitherto very limited proportion of men reaching the conscription age. Shortage of money had meant that the Russian army, though based on a population three times greater than Germany's, was no larger than Germany's, had considerably fewer guns and had considerably fewer strategic railways. That was about to change, and dramatically so. By 1914, Sir Arthur Nicolson, who had been the British ambassador in St Petersburg, was hugging himself with glee that the two countries were in alliance.

In Berlin, there was panic. It was easy in those days to find out what potential enemies were doing. Troops would have to go by train, and the length of platforms gave the game away as regards enemy war plans; there were no restrictions on travel, or photography, and an Austro-Hungarian intelligence officer even moved around south-western Russia with a passport in which his profession was entered as 'General Staff officer'. If a platform were suspiciously long, in some out-of-the-way place normally catering for farmers' wives carrying chickens, then it meant that, at some point, infantry or cavalry would be unloaded there. Then again, all countries by now had a parliament, and its proceedings were a matter of public record, to be read even in the daily press. Berlin and Vienna could therefore very easily know, by the spring of 1914, that the Russians were flexing their new economic muscle in military matters. The German Chancellor, Theobald von Bethmann Hollweg, had seen for himself the growing strength of

Russia, as the Gold Standard now supported its currency and as railways linked supply and demand at all levels. Technical journals showed the extraordinary advance of Russia – here, a lorry winning a European prize for a long journey to Riga, there a theoretical physicist (Cholkovsky) writing the equations that would eventually carry *Sputnik* (the first man-made space satellite) beyond Earth's gravity. St Petersburg still is the European capital of the might-have-been. Bethmann Hollweg was easily intelligent enough to know that Germany should just have adapted to this. He was asked by his son whether long-maturing elms should be planted on his Brandenburg estate, Hohenfinow. The Chancellor said: no, only the Russians would profit. In that, he was right: thirty years later, they did indeed arrive in Brandenburg, and stayed for another fifty. But Bethmann Hollweg himself was a fatalist, and he gave in to other men who did not have his scepticism. The military were now banging on the table: Germany could win a war now, but if she waited a further two or three years, Russia would be too strong.

The increase in the Russian army's size and weight was bad enough. What caused panic was the growth of her railways. Russia after 1908 joined in the process of self-propelling industrialization that had already occurred most spectacularly in the USA and Germany. She had of course enormous resources, but they had been poorly exploited because transport was a problem and no one trusted the paper money. That changed as railways and gold grew, and in 1909 the Tsar's chief minister, Pyotr Stolypin, told a French journalist, 'Give the state twenty years of internal and external peace and you will not recognize Russia.' The budget income had doubled by 1914, and some of the money went to build railways capable of delivering troops to the front much faster than before. Cologne commuters needed some 700 trains every day, and, as a standard of comparison, the Russian army in 1910 was to have been mobilized with 250. By 1914, that figure had risen to 360, and by 1917 it was to be 560, which would have allowed the Russians to be all present and correct on the border only three days after the completion of German mobilization. In 1917, in other words, the situation of 1945 would be foreseeable – the British in Hamburg, the Russians in Berlin, and goodbye to Bethmann Hollweg's elms.

The German generals had a preponderance in public affairs that had no equivalent elsewhere. They were now in a condition of panic. Faced with a Franco-Russian alliance, the German war plan had been obvious enough. Russia was still a backward country with far fewer railways than the western Powers – her army would only just have been mustered as the French collapsed. In such circumstances, said the Chief of the German General Staff in 1897, Count Schlieffen, the German army would have ample time to repeat the victory of 1870 against France. Then it would turn against Russia. German mobilization would be a gigantic labour – a million competent railwaymen on over 40,000 miles of double-track line with 30,000 locomotives, 65,000 passenger cars and 700,000 goods wagons were to shift, in seventeen days, 3 million soldiers, 86,000 horses and mountains of war goods, particularly guns and shell. A single army corps needed 6,000 wagons, a cavalry division 1,200. The German military had matters so organized that this force would be ready on the borders by the seventeenth day after mobilization had been declared, and for many years they could be sure that the Russians, with far fewer railways, and with much less technical capacity in the form of watering, telegraphs, coal depots, even properly sized platforms, would be much less efficient: indeed, a third of the 40,000 men in the railway battalions were illiterate. But these vital calculations were losing their very basis, and there was a further factor: Austria-Hungary, Germany's only real ally, would soon disintegrate.

The signs of that were all around. In an age of nationalism, this vast multi-national empire was an anachronism (there were fifteen versions of the imperial anthem, the *Gott Erhalte*, including a Yiddish one). Vienna had mismanaged the balancing act, and when Serbia, the leading South Slav nation, won such victories in the Balkan Wars, her example inspired much anti-Austrian political activity in the South Slav lands that Austria-Hungary ran. How was Vienna to respond? The sensible answer would have been a sort of Yugoslavia uniting all South Slavs under Vienna, which intelligent Serbs (themselves often trained in Austria-Hungary) would have supported. But the Hungarians who really ran the empire did not want another national unit, and Vienna in 1914 therefore had nothing to offer. In A. J. P. Taylor's words, Vienna waited upon events or, rather, hoped that there would be none. But there was, and it precipitated the First World War. The Austro-Hungarian foreign minister at Brest-Litovsk, Count Czernin, put it another way: 'We were bound to die. We were at liberty to choose the manner of our death and we chose the most terrible.'

On 28 June 1914 the heir to the throne, Archduke Franz Ferdinand, was assassinated in Sarajevo, capital of Bosnia, a heartland of the South Slavs. Philosophers refer to 'the inevitable accident', and this was a very accidental one. Some young Serb terrorists had planned to murder him as he paid a state visit. They had bungled the job, throwing a bomb that missed, and one of them had repaired to a café in a side street to sort himself out. The Archduke drove to the headquarters of the governor-general, Potiorek (where he was met by little girls performing folklore), and berated him (the two men were old enemies, as the Archduke had prevented the neurasthenic Potiorek from succeeding an elderly admirer as Chief of the General Staff). The Archduke went off in a rage, to visit in hospital an officer wounded by the earlier bomb. His automobile moved off again, a Count Harrach standing on the running board. Its driver turned left after crossing a bridge over Sarajevo's river. It was the wrong street, and the driver was told to stop and reverse. In reverse gear such automobiles some-times stalled, and this one did so – Count Harrach on the wrong side, away from the café where one of the assassination team was calming his nerves. Now, slowly, his target drove up and stopped. The murderer, Gavrilo

Princip, fired. He was seventeen, a romantic schooled in nationalism and terrorism, and part of a team that stretches from the Russian Nihilists of the middle of the nineteenth century, exemplified especially in Dostoyevsky's prophetic *The Possessed* and Joseph Conrad's *Under Western Eyes*. Austria did not execute adolescents and Princip was young enough to survive. He was imprisoned and died in April 1918. Before he died, a prison psychiatrist asked him if he had any regrets that his deed had caused a world war and the death of millions. He answered: if I had not done it, the Germans would have found another excuse.

In this, he was right. Berlin was waiting for 'the inevitable accident'. The army had been saying for some time that it could win a European war then and there but that it would not be manageable once Russia had established herself – 1917 being the expected date for this, when strategic railways would shuttle Russian troops back and forth at Germanic speed. Now, the potential prizes and liabilities appeared to be enormous – the disintegration of Germany's only ally; the possibility of a German empire in the Near and Middle East; the arrival of a Russian super-power. Men could have gone on talking airily about all of this for ever. But now these questions were forced upon Berlin. The maker of Germany, Bismarck, had been brilliant at seizing upon accidents and making use of them to show his enemies in the wrong light. Bismarck's statues dominated endless towns and his successors wondered how he had done it. Now, in 1914, came another accident, with the Archduke. The

Austro-Hungarian foreign ministry had been wondering how Germany could be involved. A Count Hoyos was sent to Berlin, saying: what should we do? He ran into a world that was looking for an excuse.

After the War had been lost, nearly all of the men involved destroyed their private papers – the German Chancellor, the Austro-Hungarian foreign minister, almost the whole of the German military. We really know what happened in Berlin in 1914 only from the contents of trunks, forgotten in attics, and an extraordinary document, the diary of Kurt Riezler, who was the (Jewish) secretary of Bethmann Hollweg.[5] In the diary there is a devastating entry for 7 July 1914. In the evening the young man sits with the grey-bearded Chancellor von Bethmann Hollweg. They commune, and Riezler knows, as he listens, that he is catching the hem of fate. The key line is: 'Russia grows and grows. She has become a nightmare.' The generals, says Bethmann Hollweg, all say that there must be a war before it is too late. Now, there is a good chance that it will all work out. By 1917, Germany has no hope. Therefore, now: if the Russians go to war, better 1914 than later. But the western Powers might let Russia down, in which case the Entente will split apart, and, either way, Germany will be the winner.

Injured innocence was paraded as the plot went ahead – the Kaiser off on his yacht, the foreign minister on his honeymoon, the chief of the general staff taking the waters. It was Bethmann Hollweg, on his estate, who gave the lie to it all, and in the oddest way. There was one record that was not destroyed: his expenses. They have turned up. Bethmann Hollweg went several times to Berlin, during the ostensible holiday, and, being mean, wanted the State to pay. Back and forth he went, organizing the country's finances (and maybe his own as well – he came from a banking family) for the likelihood of war, with debts to collect and bonds discreetly to sell or buy. The Warburgs in Hamburg were being told, by special courier, what to do. Berlin meant war.

A fire-eating diplomat in the Austro-Hungarian foreign ministry called the Archduke's murder 'a gift from Mars' – a wonderful excuse to solve all problems. Austria would be great again, Russia would come to heel, even Turkey might be taken over. In six weeks, a Bismarckian victory. It was, the German emperor said, 'Now or never'. War was to be provoked, and the murder of the Archduke provided a perfect occasion. The Austrians were told that they should use it to attack Serbia, Russia's client, and the means chosen was an ultimatum, containing demands that could not be accepted without the loss of Serbian independence. As it happened, the Austrians were not at all enthusiastic for war with Russia – Serbia, yes, but Russia was too great. The worries translated into delays – the Hungarians to be placated, the harvest to be brought in, and so on. Discreet banging on the table came from Berlin, and on 23 July the ultimatum was sent off. On the 25th, it was accepted but with reservations, and the Austrians declared mobilization – still no declaration of war. There was more banging of the table in Berlin, and war was declared on the 28th.

Now the challenge to Russia was clear: would she protect her Balkan position and, by extension, her future in the Ottoman empire and the Straits? At first the Tsar did not quite believe what was happening (and when the German ambassador eventually handed over his country's declaration of war, he did so in tears). Perhaps just a part of the army could be mobilized, against Austria alone? The German emperor himself had second thoughts, and there were exchanges of imperial telegrams. Towards the very end of the crisis, Chancellor Bethmann Hollweg too seems to have had doubts. But by now the German military were adamant, because they had an argument of unshakeable strength. It all depended upon railways. Railways won wars. If one power managed to get ahead with the call-up and movement – mobilization – of an army consisting of millions of men, it could reach the enemy borders before the other army was ready. That had happened in the Franco-Prussian war of 1870, when the French had made a mess of their mobilization whereas the Germans had done their staff work efficiently. The French army was in effect surrounded and captured within six weeks. There had been another railway disaster in the Russo-Japanese war of 1904–5, when these two powers had collided over China: the Trans-Siberian railway could not cope with the problems of supply, and Russia had to make peace. Now, in 1914, every general staff was worried that the rival army would start first, and the Germans insisted on full Austro-Hungarian mobilization against Russia: the 'iron dice' were supposed to 'roll'. The German military themselves clearly wanted a war, and had already decided to mobilize, but they were given a considerable present when, on 31 July, general mobilization was declared in St Petersburg just before the German announcement was made. This meant that mobilization could be presented as defensive, which, given potential opposition in the Reichstag, mattered. As things were, the Social Democrats made no problems, and voted credits for war. The German ambassador handed over a requirement for the end of Russian mobilization, and when it was refused, war was declared on 1 August. The German war plan meant an immediate attack on France, and the trains began to roll. An ultimatum was served in Paris, to the effect that the French must declare neutrality, with guarantees. When this was refused, war followed there, too, on 3 August.

There was a final twist. The German army could not really attack France directly, because the fortifications on the short Franco-German border were far too strong. It could only invade France through the plains of Belgium, and Belgium was a neutral country, her neutrality guaranteed by the Great Powers, including Great Britain and Germany. What were the British to do if Germany invaded Belgium? In terms of treaty obligations, the position could be violently interpreted: war. Winston Churchill as First Lord of the Admiralty alerted the Royal Navy at once. The situation of 1914, of war in the West emerging from some crisis in the East, had been foreseen, and study of the railways in Westphalia had even shown that there would be a German invasion of Belgium. But war between Germany and England was in many quarters unthinkable – Germany, the model country, with the largest Social Democrat party, the best local government, the best education in Europe. Why go to war with her, at the side of Tsarist Russia? But, as happened with redoubled force in 1939, reason was hardly counting. Germany had built an entirely unnecessary fleet, directed straight at British ports, and had gone on to aggressive behaviour against Russia, against France. Members of the British cabinet had quite a good idea of what it was all about, the central question of British foreign policy since 1850: Germany or Russia? What would have happened if, at the treaty of Brest-Litovsk, the then British foreign secretary had appeared, indicating that he had no objection to a German-dominated Europe, provided that British interests, worldwide, were guaranteed? The trouble was that, by then, no one trusted the Germans, and the brightest figure in British politics, David Lloyd George, said that a Germany controlling the resources of Russia would be unbeatable. Without a German invasion of Belgium, the British navy would in any event have been engaged in defending the Atlantic coast of France. The invasion of Belgium gave a cast-iron excuse for intervention, which silenced many (though not all) of the doubters. On 4 August a British ultimatum demanding the evacuation of Belgium was issued: it remained without answer, and the European war became a world war.

NOTES

1. Heinz von Lichem, *Krieg in den Alpen 1915–1918* (Augsburg, 1993), vol. 3, p. 179 ff.

2. The French had money to spare partly because, almost alone in Europe at the time, their population hardly rose between 1870 and 1914, and might-have-been parents saved with ferocity.

3. It was of course true that imperialism enriched the imperialists and their professorial hangers-on, but the costs of it were prodigious, and Weber himself learned as much. After his inaugural lecture, he became a national hero, and attracted the attentions of a very clever woman, who led him into a world of which he had had no knowledge. He was, for much of the time, a nervous wreck, and seems thereby to have learned that professor-doctors do not really have a monopoly of wisdom. He grew up. In 1914, almost all of the thousand-plus great names in German cultural life signed a 'petition of the Intellectuals' that argued on Weber-inaugural lines. Weber became a medical assistant on the western front. See Joachim Radkau, *Max Weber: Die Leidenschaft des Denkens* (Munich, 2005), pp. 215–33 and p. 548ff.

4. Hitler even took the idea of having a party uniform of special shirts from Mussolini, who had chosen black. He hit upon brown ones, by accident, when a job lot of jungle uniforms turned up on the market. They had been intended for the German army in East Africa and were stored in south-eastern Turkey, where they were acquired by an enterprising Austrian.

5. Riezler's biography is one of several Central European descants upon the history of the century. He married the daughter of the painter Max Liebermann, head (until Hitler)

of the Prussian Academy of Sciences. Riezler was a considerable philosopher (and wrote learnedly on Parmenides). He entered the German Foreign Office, in the press department, and became private secretary to Bethmann Hollweg, with whom he spent a great deal of time. When in 1917 Bethmann Hollweg fell from office, Riezler became a diplomat, arranging the arrival of Lenin in Stockholm. Then, after some rearrangement, he became associated with the Social Democrats who ran Germany in the twenties – private secretary to the Social Democrat president, Ebert – but he moved left and became professor at the neo-Marxist Frankfurt School. In 1933, he moved to the USA, to the University of Chicago, where he used his influence to defeat the candidacy for professorship of Karl Popper, then an exile (from Austria) in New Zealand. In 1945, Leo Szilard, the nuclear physicist, wanted direct contact with President Roosevelt in order to protest about the dropping of the atom bomb. He needed an introduction, and enlisted Albert Einstein, who obliged, and secured him an interview with Eleanor Roosevelt. Roosevelt himself then died, and Einstein's letter of introduction was addressed instead to Roosevelt's stand-in, Truman. President Truman set up a commission to judge the morality of dropping it. Its president? Kurt Riezler. (He advised in favour.)

WWI

previous pages: Calling up of Turkish troops in Constantinople, October 1914

In four years, the world went from 1870 to 1940. In 1914, cavalry cantered off to stirring music, the Austrian Prince Clary-Aldringen wore the uniform he had put on for a gala at Buckingham Palace, and early illustrations of the war show clumps of infantry charging with bayonets, as shrapnel explodes overhead. It is 1870. Fortresses were readied for prolonged sieges, medical services were still quite primitive, and severely wounded men were likely to die. By 1918, matters had become very different, and French generals had already devised a new method of warfare, in which tanks, infantry and aircraft collaborated, in the manner of the German *Blitzkrieg* ('lightning war') of 1940. Cavalry regiments became museum-pieces, and fortresses, relics. The war proved to be a great killer – 10 million died – but it was, as the French writer Louis-Ferdinand Céline, himself a doctor, called it, 'the vaccinated apocalypse'. Medicine made greater progress in these four years than at any time before or after: by 1918, only 1 per cent of wounded men died.

However, to begin with, illusion reigned. In 1914, to crowds of cheering people, the troops moved off, generals on horseback dreaming that they would have a statue in some square named after them. No war has ever begun with such a fundamental misunderstanding of its nature. Perhaps the deepest misunderstanding was British. On 3 August 1914 the Foreign Secretary, Sir Edward Grey, made a speech in the House of Commons that was very greatly admired and seems to have convinced many of the doubting MPs that war with Germany was right. He remarked that the country would suffer 'terribly, in this war, whether we are in it or whether we stand aside'. In retrospect, a grotesque remark.

Nearly half of the British economy, and over a third of the German, was taken up with foreign trade, much of it with the European Continent. Interruption of it was expected to bring unemployment and bankruptcy; another cabinet minister (who resigned) said that the social problems resulting from the interruption of trade would bring a variant of the revolutions of 1848, when the established order in old Europe had been swept away by upheavals in the cities. Because of the threat to trade, bankers – Sir Felix Schuster, chairman of the bankers' association for one – assured everyone that the war would have to be stopped after six months. The generals themselves knew that they had the wherewithal to go on for a very long time – millions of men and the means to feed, clothe, arm and transport them. But the bankers had another argument. How could the war be paid for? British and French credit was very strong, but Germany's public finances were surprisingly weak, as she was a federal country with many spending points. The Hungarian finance minister, a Baron Teleszky, when solemnly asked in cabinet how long he could pay for the war, replied, three weeks.[1] The gold would by then have run out (in 1914 gold-backed coinage was common) and the only alternative would be to print paper money, and that would mean inflation – grubby and crumpled notes changing hands very fast, and quickly losing their value. That in turn would make the social problems following upon the cessation of trade quite ungovernable, the poor becoming much poorer, maybe even starving. This is in fact what happened when Russia exploded in Bolshevik revolution in 1917, and Italy almost followed, with inflation of 700 per cent. The bankers were not wrong in anything other than timing.

The armies went to war, just the same, with an illusion that it would all be over very soon – 'home by Christmas'. The Russian High Command, *Stavka*, asking for new typewriters, were told that the war would not last for long enough to justify the expenditure: the old ones would have to do. Generals promised to write to their wives every day, and soon ran out of things to say. The Austro-Hungarian commander (who wrote to another man's wife) slept in an iron cot; the Russian high command ordained religious services every day and foreswore vodka, unless foreigners were present. By November, foreigners were much in demand, and the choir was singing *Prince Igor*. But to begin with the plans of every country reflected 'the short war illusion' – an immediate and vast attack, taking up resources that, with hindsight, should have been husbanded for what was to come. But other calculations, relating to fortresses, artillery and cavalry, also proved quite wrong-headed.

Northern France and Belgium were studded with fortresses, strategically placed above rivers that an invading army would have to cross – especially the long, winding, Franco-German Meuse – and their names again and again come up in military history, as far back as the Middle Ages: Liège, Namur, Maubeuge, Dinant, Verdun, Toul, Antwerp. They were very expensive and contained thousands of guns. When they were modernized in the 1880s, the usual rule was to have a very strong citadel, with a ring of forts to keep enemy artillery beyond range of it. In the 1890s, artillery ranges became longer and the shells heavier. More forts and more elaborate fortifications, usually with concrete, had to be constructed if the fortresses were to be effective. But by 1914 the guns had won. Heavy howitzers were able to launch high explosive at a range of ten miles, and the fortresses were an obvious target – a trap for the defenders, who would have been better off if they had just dug unidentifiable holes in the ground outside the forts. Earth absorbed high explosive far more easily than concrete could, however pre-stressed, and all fortresses attacked in the campaign of 1914 fell quickly. Liège, on the German border with Belgium, lasted only two days.

With cavalry, the illusion was also dispelled, but not

as dramatically. In the Crimean War the Light Brigade had charged Russian guns, and had at least been able to reach them. In 1914, this was no longer possible. An infantryman with a rifle could hit a horse a mile off, and artillery was more devastating still, at a range of three miles. However, in empty territory, cavalry was still serviceable and could find out where the enemy was; and there was not much alternative to it, because the internal combustion engine was still in a relatively un-developed stage – almost all of the fifty German lorries crossing the mountainous Ardennes broke down. But horses, eating ten kilograms of fodder every day, made huge demands on the supply-lines, and it was infantry supplies that suffered. The war in the West began with boots and saddles and bugles, with divisions of French dragoons and German Uhlans showing off. The Austro-Hungarians used a saddle that was designed to give the rider a perfect seat. In hot weather, and with horses requisitioned from civilians, it rubbed the skin on the poor beasts' backs, and the dragoons returned from their first foray into Russian territory leading them on foot. Russian cavalry probed East Prussia and fell back at once for lack of fodder, while the elderly Khan of Nakhichevan, one of the Tsar's prized Tatar cavalrymen (the Tatar cavalry had been officially thanked for putting down revolutionary troubles in Odessa in 1905), was unable to mount his horse because of piles.

The wars that Europeans remembered had been short – especially the Franco-Prussian one of 1870 – and they did not pay much attention to the American Civil War, which had been long and very bloody. Every Power therefore attacked. The Germans were first off the mark. They followed the Schlieffen Plan, a grand offensive in the west, through Belgium. The German right wing was supposed to move north-west of Paris, while the French manned the heavily fortified eastern border, and perhaps tried to invade southern Germany. The French would be trapped, hoped Schlieffen, though he had also warned (in 1905) that the plan would not work unless the army were much stronger than it was. In 1914, there were 1,700,000 men on the German side, 2,000,000 on the French, to which 100,000 British and Belgians were added. On the whole, the Germans were better prepared. If you had universal conscription, young men ate and wore most of the military budget, and there was not much left for intensive training of long-serving soldiers – non-commissioned officers (NCOs) – or even sophisticated equipment. The French used conscription as a tool to instil republican nationalism, almost half of their population being peasants who quite often did not even speak proper French. They took everyone, including monks.

The German army was able to concentrate more on training and equipment, as its general officers simply did not want to expand too far and have to use, as officers, men who would 'water down' the qualities of Prussia. They spent proportionately less on feeding conscripts; they had three times as many NCOs as the French, and far more than the Russians, where NCOs were hardly distinguished from ordinary soldiers. The

French also lacked the heavy artillery of the Germans, their own having been stuffed into fortresses, and they lacked two other weapons that the Germans understood. The first was a light mortar, able to throw a shell on a high trajectory (45°) and thus place it behind fortifications, or among trees, whereas a flat-trajectory gun (16°) would not have touched the defenders. The other weapon was the spade, otherwise known as an entrenching tool. Soldiers in a hole in the ground were very difficult to spot, and were almost invulnerable except to heavy shelling. The Germans had spades, the French did not. Why, is a good question: the answer is probably that the Germans, training their fewer men more intensively, could rely upon them not to panic, whereas the French, training more men with fewer NCOs, meant to keep them moving forward in simple, even crude, large formations (similar to the columns of the Revolutionary Wars a century before, which had also been far more costly in lives than the eighteenth-century linear formations). That the men were clothed in red and blue made them very conspicuous as well, whereas all other armies had gone over to dull-coloured uniforms; even the Scottish regiments' kilts were khaki.

Off the armies went, and the first move was German. The great fortress of Liège had to be taken if the Germans were to pass through Belgium easily – they needed the railways, and Liège was the key. On 7 August they took the central citadel by a ruse, and the outer forts then fell to Austrian heavy guns that had been specially brought in. By 18 August the German concentration was complete, and a huge force entered the Belgian plains. There were three armies – three quarters of a million men, in fifty-two divisions – their left flank fixed in the Lorraine fortifications around Metz and Thionville. There were weaker forces further south, along the Franco-German border.

In effect the three German armies were moving into undefended space, and they marched fast – twenty miles a day, an extraordinary achievement. The Belgians just withdrew to their other two fortresses – the Antwerp complex, on the sea, and Namur. There was a French army (Lanrezac's Fifth) south of that area, and the British Expeditionary Force was forming up to its left, but there were no engagements for some time. The French commander, Joseph Joffre, was not as concerned as he might have been, because he was staging what he regarded as a gigantic counter-offensive over the German border – Plan XVII, by which the Germans were supposed to be driven back to the Rhine, over Alsace and Lorraine. This was a disaster. On 20 August, at Morhange-Sarrebourg, French troops were shattered as they charged uphill into machine-guns; then they were attacked, and lost 150 guns and 20,000 men as prisoners. On 21 August Joffre tried again, this time in the Ardennes, the hilly and wooded area of north-eastern France and south-eastern Belgium. It was the German centre, and since there had been such evidence of strength on the German right and left, the centre was supposed to be weak. There was another disaster, as the French ran into a force of their own size, but one equipped with the sort of artillery that could deal with fighting in woods, whereas the French standard gun, the 75 mm, was ineffective in that terrain. Further to the north-west Lanrezac's army also did badly, and began to retreat away from Namur. It lost touch with the British, whose commander, Sir John French, waxed irascible. On 23 August the right-hand German army, Kluck's First, ran into the British on the Mons–Conde canal, and British regulars, firing one round every four seconds, held off considerably superior numbers, inflicting three times the 1,850 losses they themselves suffered. In the afternoon, German howitzers arrived to deal with the difficult situation and the British retreated, parallel with Lanrezac's army. The French had lost heavily – 75,000 killed by the end of August, with a further 200,000 losses in wounded and prisoners. The Germans had lost far fewer, and they were coming in fast from the north, without much opposing them. A great Franco-British retreat started, with a view to a regrouping around Paris.

It was well managed: at no stage were guns captured, and no German encirclement threatened. Losses were at once made up, and the French had a huge advantage, in that the railways behind their lines could shuttle troops from the south-east to the north-west far faster than the Germans could follow on foot. The Germans had had only 4,000 lorries, and two thirds of them broke down before the retreat ended; besides, the Meuse bridges had been destroyed, and the Belgians had sabotaged their railways and most of the tunnels: only 400 miles of the 2,500-mile network were back in operation by early

September. Ammunition was a priority for the horse-transport, and the horses themselves could only be fed on green corn, which made them sick. Kluck's army had 84,000 horses, and the beasts dropped dead at the side of the road, so there were delays in the hauling of heavy guns. What with the troops' exhaustion in the August heat, some units were down to half their nominal strength. There was a further headache with communications. Moltke, back in Koblenz, was too far away, and wireless worked very clumsily as well as openly: the French could listen in. There was a system of limited decentralization in the German army which enabled what seems in retrospect to have been an almost miraculous advance, but generals quite often did not really know what their neighbours were doing. Between 5 and 9 September, as the battle of the Marne was being fought, the German High Command issued no orders at all, and on the last two days received no reports. There were other problems, of troops being taken away from the decisive front for purposes that also seemed essential – two corps for Antwerp and Maubeuge, and two further ones for East Prussia; Namur also occupied troops. Moltke wasted effort by ordering his left-wing armies to attack, which they ineffectually did towards Nancy, rather than shifting them to the right. On 27 August he ordered a more-or-less general advance, with the two right-wing armies moving towards the lower Seine and Paris, and then on 2 September altered this so that they moved east of Paris, the right-hand one, Kluck's First, crossing to the south-east, across the northern side of the city. This change happened in part because Kluck's neighbour to the east, Bülow's Second Army, had been checked by the French Fifth at Guise, and Kluck himself had run into quite serious British resistance at Le Câteau (26 August), and so the German right was bunched closer together and the sweep west of Paris was abandoned.

Joffre at this moment was keeping his nerve better than Moltke. He meant to raise fresh troops and to shift others from the eastern side to the west, where a new army could attack Kluck's open right-hand flank. These movements started on 25 August. There were initial problems with the British: Sir John French proposed more or less to withdraw from the battle and prepare for return to England, if necessary. French was browbeaten only when Lord Kitchener arrived in full-dress Field Marshal's uniform to order him to conform with the French plans. Meanwhile, a new French coalition government insisted on defence of the capital, and it was strengthened by troops intended for the new army to the north-west. When on 3 September Kluck turned east from Paris to keep his links to Bülow's army, the way was open for a stroke against his western flank. Between the capital and Verdun, there was a further German advance, over the river Marne, though it did not lead anywhere: attacks were exchanged by the German Second Army and Foch's new Ninth, in the marshes of St Gond. On 4 September Joffre ordered an attack on the 6th from the Paris and Verdun sides, but fighting started the day before, when the new French army on the western side (Sixth) clashed on the river Ourcq with part of Kluck's forces: it was then that troops were ferried from Paris by taxi – a great patriotic legend, though the taxis kept their meters running. With some difficulty this attack was held, but Kluck marched two of his corps from his own left wing back towards the right, and this meant that a gap opened up between his and Bülow's armies, roughly between the Grand and Petit Morin rivers, tributaries that flowed from the south into the Marne.

Just before the gap, by chance, stood the British Expeditionary Force, and it moved forward, cautiously, into almost empty space, driving a wedge between the two armies of the German right. In general, the German armies on the right were now considerably inferior to the forces that the Allies now had – twenty divisions to thirty – and, besides, the Germans were running out of ammunition, whereas the French were learning to use their field guns more sensibly. On 8 September there was a staff conference at Moltke's headquarters and an Intelligence colonel went off by motor-car to interview Kluck and Bülow. He discovered that Bülow had decided to withdraw if the British crossed the Marne, which, on the 9th, fliers reported had happened. Kluck would have to retreat accordingly, though he did not wish to. Moltke, his courage failing, visited other army commanders on 11 September and ordered the Third, Fourth and Fifth Armies, to the east, also to withdraw. Between 9 and 14 September the Germans fell back to a chalk ridge rising 500 feet above the river Aisne, and the infantry were ordered to fortify the position. Troops dug in, with barbed wire defences, could not easily be spotted by artillery and were invulnerable to rifles; they could only be dislodged by hand-grenades, and these had to be thrown from close to. Joffre supposed that the Germans were on the run, and his men were made to attack, despite exhaustion, bad weather and lack of munitions. Allied attacks on the Aisne positions therefore got nowhere, and by the end of September that part of the front was fixed – a stalemate.

The French had had great hopes of Russian victory; money had been invested in strategic railways, the doubling of tracks and the lengthening of platforms. One outcome was that Russian mobilization did proceed as the Germans had feared, and there were large numbers of soldiers on the East Prussian border by mid-August, though all sorts of ancillary services were not yet available to back them up. As they had promised, the Russians invaded East Prussia with some thirty divisions, in two armies, the First, moving west, and the Second, some way to the south-west, moving north from Warsaw. In theory, they should have been able to trap the single German army, the Eighth, as it concentrated on the eastern border and the fortress of Königsberg, but the theory was difficult to realize. The two Russian armies were separated by a region of lakes and forest, where troops would not be easy to spot, and the Russian cavalry was quite ineffective, for lack of supplies, almost as soon as it crossed the border. Besides, there were railways available to the Germans, running east–west, whereas the Russians could only march forward from Grodno or Warsaw, shuffling through the dust of August roads. The Russian situation was difficult again, because communications were exceedingly poor, such that telegrams had to be brought up from Warsaw by motorcar, in bundles. Samsonov, commanding the Russian Second Army, had nearly twenty divisions, infantry and cavalry, and it was difficult for these even to keep in communication with each other, let alone with another army; Russian orders were broadcast over the radio without even being encoded, since that took too long, and there were not the non-commissioned officers who could be trusted with the task. German Intelligence therefore knew everything that was going on.

Still, the Germans began badly. Their Eighth Army had thirteen divisions, and its obvious tactic was to strike at one of the two Russian armies before the other could join up with it. On 20 August the Germans staged a frontal attack on the eastern invaders – the First Army – and lost 8,000 men (of 30,000 attackers) in an afternoon. On 22 August the commander, von Prittwitz, panicked, gabbling out to Moltke on the telephone that he would have to give up East Prussia and fall back on the great river Vistula. He was dismissed, and a retired general, Paul von Hindenburg, took over, with, as chief of staff, Erich Ludendorff, known before the war as an energetic organizer; he had also shown panache at Liège. They were a good team. Ludendorff was very competent, but praise went to his head, and he could lose a sense of proportion. Hindenburg was the foot on the brake, though he sometimes referred to himself ironically as 'the shop sign'. The important thing was for the new commanders to keep their heads, as the Russian Second Army struggled northwards in the rear of their own forces, worsted in the frontier battle to the east. These forces were pulled back – part by rail, transferred to the western side of the Russian Second Army, and part by foot along paths that led straight towards the eastern flank of that same army. It, meanwhile, plodded forward without any idea of what was happening. The First Army was told to busy itself with the fortress city of Königsberg, on the Baltic shores, and therefore subtracted itself altogether from proceedings concerning the Second Army. On 24 August the Second Army collided with the Germans, and for a time its centre made progress – illusory progress, as the further it moved north the more of it would be caught in the two arms of the German flank attacks. On the 26th, the western one moved, striking through a disordered and bewildered Russian left, and cutting its communications. Next day, the eastern one caught the Russian right, and its advance-guards met up with the other enveloping troops from the west. In the middle of the entrapment were four Russian army corps, the troops running short of everything, their commanders quite baffled as to what was happening. In packets, they surrendered on 28 August – almost 100,000 men (with 50,000 killed and wounded) and 500 guns – and their commander shot himself. It was an enormous defeat, the most spectacular of the war, and it became a legend. There was a village not far off,

Tannenberg, where in the Middle Ages the Teutonic
Knights had been defeated by Slavs. That village gave its
name to the battle, and 'Tannenberg' became a symbol
of Germanic pride. It also gave Hindenburg and Ludendorff a reputation that lasted to the very end of the war,
and even beyond. The Tannenberg monument was quite
close to Hitler's wartime headquarters at Rastenburg,
both of them later blown up by Russians or Poles.

The Russians withdrew back over the borders, narrowly
defeating a German effort to penetrate the eastern one,
in the lakes of Masuria, and there was a pause on the
Russo-German front. However, there was some compensation for the Russians, because against Austria-
Hungary they did well. The agony of the Habsburg
empire was beginning. Over fifty Russian infantry and
eighteen cavalry divisions were being mustered in
southern Poland and the western Ukraine by the end of
August, and the Austro-Hungarian forces were considerably weaker – thirty divisions to begin with, and eight
more to come from the Balkans. In artillery, they were
weaker than Russian divisions. They were also victims
of collapsing-empire syndrome, otherwise known as
'overstretch' – the contest between pride and reality.

The Austro-Hungarian commander, Franz Conrad
von Hötzendorf,[2] was a clever man. He knew that his
forces (in all, not even fifty infantry divisions, which
received less money – £25,000,000 – than the British
six) were too weak to deal with Russia, quite apart from
Serbia, the army of which was roughly one quarter the

size of Austria-Hungary's. He had an undertaking with Moltke that he would use nearly all of his army against Russia, while Germany dealt with France. However, the war with Serbia was undeniably popular, and his forces would be strong enough to deal with that if the Russians were not, at once, an effective threat. Without telling the Germans, he arranged for the armies destined for the Russian front to 'detrain' (as the British army calls it) along the Carpathian mountains, a hundred miles from the border. The Russians could toil through the plains of Galicia, southern Poland, the Germans in East Prussia would perhaps move into northern Poland, and meanwhile the other half of the Austro-Hungarian army would settle the hash of the Serbians. Conrad could always explain to the Germans that this situation had long been foreseeable – that war would come about between Austria-Hungary and Serbia, and that the Russians would be slow to make up their minds, so that the mobilization of Austria-Hungary would probably have been decided against Serbia in the first instance. This was not really a very plausible excuse, the war minister himself subsequently admitting that no one had had any real doubts as to whether Russia would intervene. Provoking her was Berlin's reason for the war. When the Germans heard what was happening, they protested, in a bombardment of messages, from the Kaiser downwards.

Conrad had to explain that the troops had already set off for the Balkans – in German eyes, an absurd misuse of a Great Power's troops at the start of a world war. Could they be re-routed? He asked his railway experts, and they were appalled: how could trains be re-routed along single-track lines in the middle of a general mobilization? The railways in Austria-Hungary reflected the fact that it was a multi-national empire, each people having to be bought off with this or that impractical concession. To stop Austrian goods reaching Hungary, for example, nineteen lines ended in buffers on the Austro-Hungarian border, and you had to travel from Austrian Slovenia, a few miles from Hungarian Croatia, either by a picturesque mountain railway or, more quickly, via Budapest. There were still private lines, and the railway in Bosnia had a different gauge, so that everything had to be transhipped on the border, at Bosnisch-Brod. The railway experts said that the mobilization against Serbia, already ordained, would have to take its course, but once the troops had detrained in the Balkans they could be loaded back into their trains and taken to the Russian front. The railwaymen were probably exaggerating, not too many of the troops of the four army corps in question having, in fact, left Prague and Budapest when Russian mobilization occurred. The experts did behave with paralysing caution, knowing that if anything went wrong there could be a disaster (railway-management was a key to this war, the German official history devoting two of its eleven volumes to the subject). They even decreed that, to avoid any possible snarl-up, all trains were to move at what they called 'maximum parallel graphic', by which was meant the maximum speed of the worst train on the worst line – ten miles per hour. Anything else, and the pins on the maps would have become hopelessly jumbled, with watering, coal and telegrams in a mess. It is true that even the best-run railways could go wrong – on the lines of the French *Nord* there was an accident every day, and it is true that great rows occurred between the British and French later on as to management of the same network. Still, the Austro-Hungarian railway experts' caution meant that mobilization occurred at a speed less than that of a decent bicycle.

With one of his armies proceeding in the wrong direction, Conrad now reinstated the original plan for deployment in southern Poland. But the railway time-tables again could not be improvised, and three other armies were detrained in the Carpathian stations, having then to be marched forward for a hundred miles in August heat. The other army – the Second – did get out on the Serbian border, stayed in tents for a while, became sucked into a failed action, and was then reloaded and taken across southern Hungary, arriving in Galicia nearly five weeks after the war had started. Once there it did not flourish. The first consequence of all this was that the grandly proclaimed offensive against Serbia failed. The commander, Potiorek – a neurotic homo-sexual and Conrad's rival, with good court connections – communicated with his chief of staff only in barely readable notes and was smarting from his failure to protect the Archduke. Moving over almost trackless mountains, slightly inferior in number to the Serbs and, unlike them, entirely inexperienced in war, the two Austro-Hungarian armies were too widely separated.

The left-hand one was overwhelmed (16–19 August), causing both to withdraw. Other efforts, up to December, similarly failed.

On the north-eastern front, two Austro-Hungarian armies were ready by 21 August, somewhat before the Russians, and there were engagements on the northern border with Russian Poland, where the Austrians did quite well, forcing back two Russian armies at more or less the same moment as the Germans captured most of the Eighth Army. However, the success was gained at the expense of the eastern part of this front. Here, one Austro-Hungarian army, the Third, stood on a river not far from the Russian border, and the missing Second army from Serbia came in only on 8 September. Overall, the Russian superiority of numbers was 750,000 to 500,000, with proportions even greater in artillery and machine guns; and that superiority had been concentrated on the eastern side. The single Austro-Hungarian army made matters worse for itself by attacking, and it was soon overwhelmed, the Russians entering the provincial capital, Lvov (German name Lemberg, by which this battle is known overall), on 3 September. Austro-Hungarian counter-strokes failed, and a general retreat was ordered, to the Carpathian foothills and the outskirts of Cracow, far to the west.

The war's pattern had been set: in the west a stalemate, and in the east a more or less constant Austro-Hungarian crisis. How should Germany, her resources only now being properly mobilized, respond? Moltke's nerves had collapsed, and he was replaced by a less hysterical figure, the Prussian minister of war, Erich von Falkenhayn. At first, there was no particular reason to panic. There had been enormous losses but, even so, troops would simply be brought back to the right level of numbers and they would try again. By now, it was clear enough that if troops attacked frontally, they would be met by a hail of shell and small-arms fire from positions in the ground that guns could not easily deal with. Both sides in France therefore tried moving into what was still an open flank, north-west of the Aisne lines, one of the oldest manoeuvres in warfare, because attackers on a flank could fire from the side at unprotected defenders who would be 'enfiladed', i.e. caught in a vulnerable line that would not be able to fire back. The trouble was that the attackers in these cases were not able to move fast enough, and there was also a lack of artillery. From mid September the clashes went on, further and further to the north-west, resulting in trench-lines that finally reached the sea on the coast of Flanders. The medieval town of Ypres was defended by the British against a formidable German attack, designed to clear Belgium altogether, as new troops came in on the German side raised principally from the oldest school pupils and from student volunteers. In late October and the first half of November, a very bloody battle went on, the British holding grimly on to the town and the subsequently famous area of 'the Ypres salient'. A salient was a part of the line that jutted out into enemy territory, and defenders were exceedingly vulnerable to fire from three sides. It would have been sensible to withdraw to a safer position, but public opinion had been whipped up to such an extent that such withdrawals would have been seen as a confession of defeat. The battle cost each side 130,000 casualties. It marked the end of the old British regular army (60,000), and the Belgians lost a third of their remaining army. For the Germans it was the 'massacre of the innocents', these hardly trained student volunteers whose units in some cases lost 60 per cent of their strength. They have 25,000 graves in the German cemetery at Langemarck.

Both sides started to develop the trench-lines, and they became more and more formidable. The front-line troops lived in 'dug-outs', underground dormitories and storehouses that were built into the trench-wall facing the enemy, for protection from shelling. Belts of barbed wire were placed in front of the line, which was also constructed in such a way as to avoid enfilading fire, i.e. in a zig-zag. Communications trenches, also zig-zagging their way back to a safer area with hospitals and supplies, were needed, and in time several lines of trenches might be dug, in case of retreat. In wet weather the trenches became very muddy, and duck-boards were used; there was also a great problem with vermin – rats fed on the corpses, and lice flourished in uniforms (a Turkish practice of placing a jacket on an ant-hill was followed, because the ants ate the lice, though their own stings were formidable). This situation of stalemate marked the entire western front by mid November 1914. In military terms it was not entirely new. In the past, besiegers and besieged had often held each other off for months, and Marlborough's campaigns in much the same territory had been very slow-moving. What was new about the situation of 1914 was its scale: millions of men, far better supplied and cared for than troops of the past, were completely immobilized in lines that were perhaps a hundred yards apart. On the whole, the Germans held the high ground and were therefore able to dig deeper before reaching the water-table, which in Flanders was quite close to the surface, the whole place having been rescued from the sea by competent medieval drainage. British troops, untrained volunteers, stumbled around in the sticky mud that was so well remembered as the main feature of the British part of the western front.

In the east, conditions were somewhat different. The front, almost a thousand miles, was twice as long, but there were fewer troops. In theory, Russia should have been able to draw upon countless millions of men, her population of 170 million being almost twice that of Germany and Austria-Hungary put together. But conscripts cost money, and the Russian war budget could not stretch to feeding and clothing more than a quarter of the available manpower. Men were therefore exempted on various grounds – religion, physical standards, drawing the long straw in a lottery. The largest exemption occurred because of 'family status'. If a man was a 'bread-winner' he did not join the army. Early in August, 2 million peasants got married, to the bewilderment of the War Ministry, which could only imagine that they intended to do their patriotic duty by producing children. The Russian first-line army, at 5 million, was no greater than the German, and on the eastern front there were generally some ninety Russian divisions to some eighty German and Austro-Hungarian ones. There were 1,500 Russians per mile of front, as against 5,000 Frenchmen, and the latter were much better armed. There was more. In the west, there were railways to transport men relatively quickly to some threatened part of the front. In Russian Poland, such railways were far fewer, and the movement of reserves was always a difficult business: at one stage, in October 1914, the High Command more or less lost a whole army, milling around the streets of Warsaw. In these circumstances, the eastern war remained one of movement, though the movement itself was generally meaningless.

In mid September the Germans realized that they would have to do something to save their ally's position. Ludendorff came to see Conrad, and at this stage, as a north German farmer's son, he was still easily awed by the grandeur of the Habsburgs, the more so as Austro-Hungarian headquarters had been moved away from the barracks of Przemysl to considerably more comfortable arrangements on a small estate at Teschen belonging to the nominal commander, Archduke Friedrich, and his wife, a Princess Croy (known as 'Busabella'). He charged rent for its use, and Conrad himself was from time to time preoccupied with organizing a Hungarian and Protestant divorce for the love of his life, whom he could not have married under Austrian (and Catholic) law. Conrad persuaded Ludendorff that the Austro-Hungarian army was in its then dreadful condition because it had been holding off the Russians so that Germany would win in the west. The condition was indeed dreadful. It had lost half a million men, 100,000 of them captured, and Przemysl, the great fortress on the northern slopes of the Carpathians, had been shut in, with a garrison of 120,000. No doubt it could have collapsed, as every other fortress did, but the mud all around was so thick that the Russians could not manoeuvre their heavy artillery, of which, in any event, they had too little. Still, there was clearly an Austro-Hungarian emergency, and a German army with Ludendorff in charge was moved to positions north of Cracow. There followed two months of manoeuvring, not unimpressive on the map, but leading nowhere. Ludendorff said that he would have done better had he had more troops.

However, Falkenhayn had to consider much more than the east. Early in November, the war took on a properly worldwide scale. Its origins had had much to do with the position of the Ottoman empire, in fact the entire Middle East, including Persia. Turkey in general was seen as backward, ripe for takeover by the Europeans, who had a new-found interest in the oil of Mesopotamia (Iraq); the Christian minorities might be used as their agents. One or two men who knew the Turks understood that they were not at all a write-off, but not many had such understanding. In 1914, Churchill commandeered two battleships being built in Newcastle, on public subscription, for the Turkish navy.

Two German battleships, *Goeben* and *Breslau*, reached Turkish waters, and adopted Turkish service: public opinion in Turkey became very pro-German. But in any case a pro-German element had seized control of Turkey. Enver Pasha, the Minister of War, and nephew-in-law of the Sultan, was producing, along with other 'Young Turks', a species of nationalism. Its model was French revolutionary and the 'Young Turks' followed the victorious Balkan-Christian states: a new language, a new interpretation of history, an exclusively national future. Enver and his closest colleague, Talat, Minister of the Interior, tricked their own government into war. Formally they took over the two German ships and, with crews wearing fezzes and pretending to be Turks, bombarded Russian ports in the expectation that the Russians would declare war. They did, early in November, and much of the Ottoman cabinet resigned in protest at Enver's provocation. But Turkey had entered the war. Enver invaded Russia, via the Caucasus, and suffered an enormous reverse – 100,000 of his men died from disease or cold in the high plateau around Sarikamiş. A German commander, Kress von Kressenstein, suffered another reverse at Suez. To Enver, this did not really matter: a Turkish nation would be born in the suffering, and it would look to Turkey proper rather than to the Arabic world. This calculation was, in the outcome, successful, though it cost Turkey one quarter of her population and was carried out, not by Enver, but by a much greater man, his rival Kemal Atatürk.

NOTES

1. At a more mundane level but expressing the same illusion, the Prague journalist Egon Erwin Kisch declined his mother's offer of spare underwear as he went off to the front: did she think it was going to be a Thirty Years War?
2. The surname is 'Conrad', by which he is properly called. 'Von Hötzendorf' is an addition, a predicate indicating nobility.

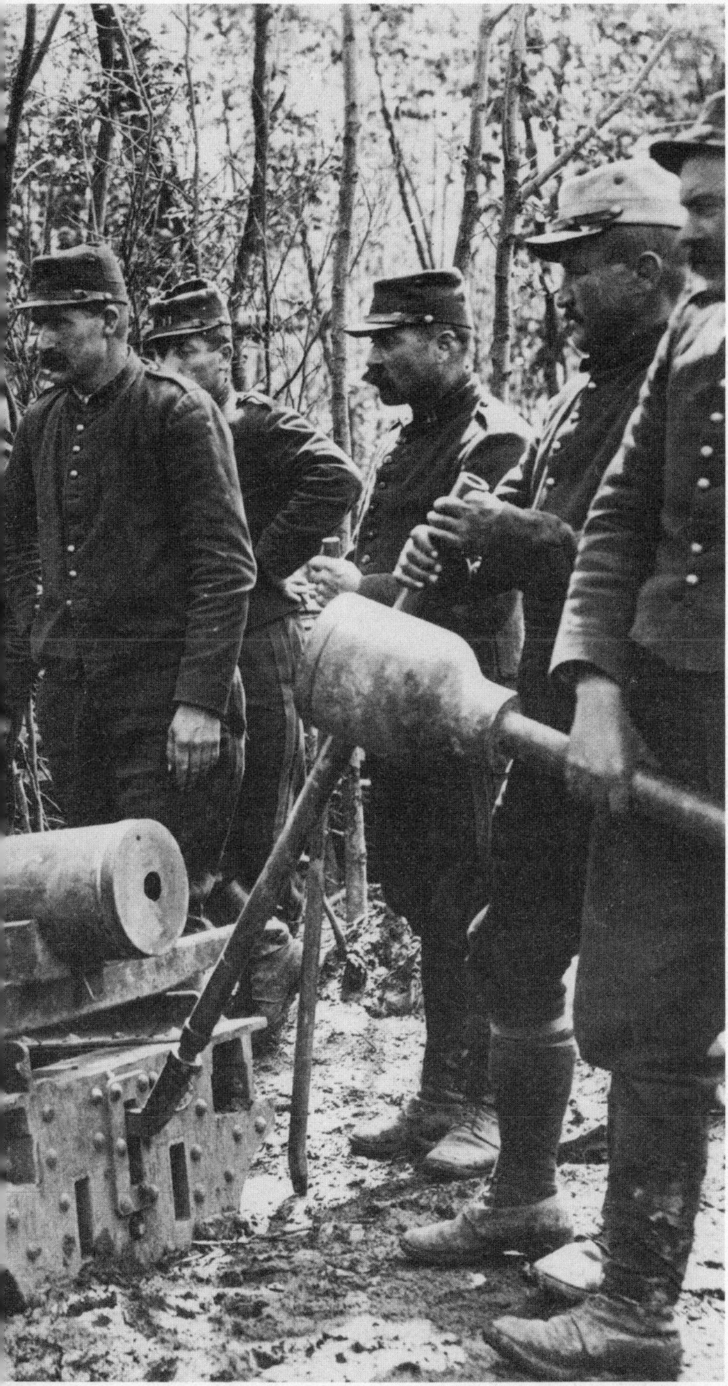

WWI

THREE · 1915

preceding pages: French 220 cannon on the Western Front, 1915

As the Ypres fighting died away and a winter freeze gripped the east, the British took stock. How was this war to be won? History was supposed to be a guide, and here the lessons were clear enough. In Napoleonic times, there had been a strategy to take account of British strengths and French weaknesses. The Royal Navy operated a blockade of French trade with the outside world, and throttled it. Brest, Bordeaux, Toulon withered on the vine, and the French influence on the world collapsed. Substitute industries, taking a great deal of money, were promoted by Napoleon, but they were not efficient, and the French economy was distorted, while French dependencies resented the blackmail of buying indifferent goods at high prices. Meanwhile, since the British monopolized overseas trade, they made a great deal of money, and they could present this, as loans, to Austrians and Russians who did the land fighting. In time, they themselves could mount a considerable military force in the furthest-flung part of Napoleon's empire, Spain – 80,000 men, by the standards of the time a large force, supplied by sea whereas the French had to supply their own response up hill and down dale over the most barren and difficult part of Europe, beset by bandits of great determination and savagery. Our word *guerrilla* – 'little war' – comes from this time. It was not in reality so 'little'. The British and the Spaniards and the Portuguese mounted an effort that was very considerable, but it was five years before the French were cleared from Spain. Napoleon called it 'the Spanish ulcer', draining his strength, but it was more than an ulcer: it was two Atlantic empires, even three if you include Portugal, against him.

Now, with enormous British naval superiority, was there not some way round the stalemate in the west? Bright sparks wondered, especially Winston Churchill, with his extraordinary quickness and imagination, his wit, his old-fashioned grand accent, his sense of English history. The navy, under his direction as First Lord of the Admiralty – a singularity of British history was that civilians controlled the armed forces, whereas in Germany they took their orders from the military – had mobilized early. Eighteen miles of grey battleships resulted, bow to stern, a sign to the Germans that, if this went on, they would collapse. In fact the first shots fired in the Anglo-German war were in Sydney Harbour Bay, in Australia, when, on 4 August, a German trader tried to leave and was warned off. A blockade of Germany was declared. However, Churchill's historical sense was deceptive in this case.

The chief aim was to stop German exports. Maurice

Hankey – Kurt Riezler's equivalent in the British machine before 1914, a formidable man, a linguist interested in everything, manager of government business at the highest level, and also responsible like Riezler for the nuclear bomb twenty years later (German Jewish exiles delivered the secret to him in 1940, and he passed it on to the Americans) – said that Germany would be destroyed if her exports were stopped. Here he was, like many other clever people, quite wrong. Nine hundred German merchantmen were picked up, and the Royal Navy (not without trouble) picked up various enemy warships around the world, including the Falkland Islands. However, if Germany were prevented from exporting, the spare machinery and labour simply went into war work. There were no riots in Hamburg – on the contrary, the great trusts which ran German industry went over to the production of war goods, the banks which were their own creatures financed this, and the Prussian War Ministry knew how to maintain quality control without getting in the way, as its British counterpart did. The effect of the British block on German exports was therefore that the German war economy did better than all others in 1915. The Russians took a year to catch up.

There was another paradox to the blockade: it became a wonderful alibi for bad management of food supplies in Germany. The British were greatly hated, blamed for scarcities that were not truly of their making. Stopping German imports was not easy because they could go through neutral ports, and in any case international law (the Declaration of London in 1909) did not allow for stoppages of food imports (even barbed wire counted only as 'conditional contraband' because it had agricultural uses). Under the British rules, neutral ships were supposed to be open for inspection, and sometimes their cargo was confiscated, which, again and again, made for problems with the USA – problems uneasily resolved by offers of post-war compensation. But there was no real way of stopping food imports through (especially) Holland.

It was true that, as the war went on, German food supplies declined, in the winter of 1916–17 quite drastically. The blockade was blamed for this. But the price-control system had more to do with it: grain was controlled, and meat was not, so farmers fed grain to their beasts. In fact grain, directly eaten, gives four times more energy than if eaten indirectly through meat (the two-pound Victorian loaf was enough for a working man's day). Then in Germany meat prices were controlled, such that the beasts were slaughtered (9 million pigs in the spring of 1915), rather than sold. There was less manure and thence a smaller harvest. Matters were made worse by the failure of the potato crop, and the winter of 1916–17 was known as 'the turnip winter', but the heart of the problem lay in blundering price-controls. The Prussian ministry of agriculture seems to have regarded the blockade as just a heightened form of the agricultural tariff which the Right had always advocated. At any rate, peasants did quite well, while the towns ate turnips and endlessly boiled sugar beet to produce a sweet syrup, which is still eaten with potato-cakes – *Reibekuchen mit Rübenkraut* – at Christmas markets in Cologne.

There was another somewhat perverse effect of the blockade, this time one that had been foreseen but misunderstood. As German exports went down, British ones were expected to take their place: the Latin American market could be recaptured, or so it was supposed. Profits from such exports could be recycled, via war loans or taxation, to the Treasury, and that in turn would mean lending money to allies, such as Italy or Russia, who would do the land fighting. There was, again, some precedent for this: in the Seven Years War of 1756–63, British money had kept Frederick the Great's Prussia going against France, Russia and Austria, while the British liquidated almost all of the French empire. Now, exports did rise – in 1916–17 to a value of £527,000,000, as against an average of £474,000,000 in the five years before the war. That figure was not equalled until 1951, and it is a curious fact that 1916 was the only year in the whole of statistically recorded time when the British sold more goods overseas than they bought. However, exports took skilled labour, diverting it (and machinery) from war work, and the whole business was bedevilled by another phenomenon characteristic of the time, that vast numbers of the skilled men volunteered for the army, so exporters faced labour-shortage and bid against each other with ever-higher wages. This problem was solved, only partially, when conscription was imposed in 1916: under conscription, exemptions could be made for essential crafts (to the extent that conscription in the end netted fewer men than the earlier volunteering had done). In 1915 these confusions affected the British war economy, and there was a serious lack of munitions in the spring and summer, whereas the Germans had been forced into a more appropriate approach. Blockade therefore turned into a set of elliptical billiard balls, and was not really properly used until 1918, when the various neutrals, mainly because of American intervention, could be coerced into limiting their trade with Germany.

But there was a further precedent (and this was an age when men were very taken with historical precedents): 'the soft under-belly' – in Napoleon's time, Spain; now, Turkey?

Turkey's intervention had turned out very badly. The Germans had had high hopes that all Islam would rise against the British, once 'holy war' was declared by the Sultan-Caliph. In most places, the appeal went into waste-paper baskets, both Russian Tatars and Indian Muslims making no trouble at all; in any case, 'holy war' made very little sense if it meant taking one set of Christians as allies against another set of Christians (and, true to form for the Young Turks, their own religious leader was anyway a Freemason from a grand Istanbul family). The Ottoman army had lost heavily in the Caucasus, and there were already signs of a revolt in the Arab provinces. A British push into the Levant might just finish off the Turks, and the Straits would be opened again for trade with Russia. The Balkan states and Italy might be encouraged to join in the war on the Allied side. Late in 1914, the British offered Constantinople to the Russians, and went on to plan for partition of the entire Ottoman empire among various allies. No one expected the Turks to be capable of serious resistance.[1] They had almost no armaments industry, and though German help could arrive through corrupt Romanians on the Danube, it was little and tardy. The Aegean, for a classically educated generation of public schoolboys, such as the poet Rupert Brooke, had its attractions, and, for Churchill, it had the great advantage of not being the western front. There were surplus British battleships, dating back to the days before 1906, when the all-big-gun *Dreadnought* made earlier ships obsolete. These could, it was imagined, sweep into the Dardanelles, the ancient Hellespont, which, only 800 yards in width, had been swum, Sestos to Abydos, in Greek mythology and then by Lord Byron.

On 18 March sixteen battleships met disaster. Their guns were not suitable against the shore batteries, and the Turks had mobile batteries as well; in any case, minefields were unswept. Three battleships were sunk, and three were put out of action. Later, once German submarines arrived, two more were sunk and the fleet had to move from offshore waters in May. The naval commander was always prudent, and expected a land force to cope with the shore defences. But that force had its base in Egypt, and even then there were delays – the supply ships were loaded in the wrong order, and the commander, Sir Ian Hamilton, sent them back to be reloaded in the right order. Malaria became a problem (it killed Rupert Brooke), and in cheese-paring fashion the army, here and in Mesopotamia, did not even provide mosquito-screens for the windows. The Greek island of Lemnos was the forward base, and preparations were all too obvious. But even the Anatolian railways and roads could deliver troops and guns to Gallipoli far more efficiently than could ships, of which fifty were needed for a single division, and seven weeks went by before the landings – weeks well used by the Turks.

Faced with what was a deadly threat, the Turks resolved on a fatal step. There had been an Armenian rising in the east, at Van, where the Muslim town was destroyed with much slaughter. Just before the British landing, Enver and Talat ordered the deportation of the Armenian population from the whole country, except Istanbul and Izmir, on the grounds that its loyalty was mainly dubious. Appeals by the Tsar, the Patriarch in Russian Armenia, several prominent Anatolian Armenians, and, finally, rebellions just behind the front line convinced the Young Turks that they must take desperate measures. The Armenians had for generations counted as 'the most loyal' of the minorities, and even in 1914 their leader, Boghos Nubar, was offered a place in the government (he refused on the grounds that his Turkish was not up to it). Scenes of great cruelty ensued, as at least 700,000 people were marched or crammed into trains towards northern Syria, to camps where a great many died of starvation and disease. There were well-documented massacres along the way.

On 25 April, Allied troops were landed at five beaches around the south-western tip of the Gallipoli Peninsula, but they were outnumbered (five divisions to six) and the naval artillery was inaccurate against concealed field guns, or for that matter just in general. The British lost heavily during the landings, and then found the terrain very difficult – wooded, and uphill, with British positions dominated by Turks on the slopes further up. The Australian and New Zealand volunteer force had a particularly challenging area – 'Anzac Cove' – but both sides dug trenches and staged frontal assaults. Even water was a problem for the invaders, as it had to be rowed in, each boat carrying none too much and usually vulnerable to fire from the dominating slopes. In August, with three fresh divisions, the British tried a landing further north, along the coast at Suvla Bay, and that, too, failed – the troops did not move inland very far, although for a time they were unopposed, because the elderly commander wanted to make sure all stores were properly landed before proceeding. Meanwhile the Turks, far from collapsing, put up a display of extraordinary resilience, one young commander, Kemal (the later) Atatürk, making his national reputation in this battle. Eventually the government in London lost faith in the whole enterprise, and the expedition was brought to a (professionally managed) end early in January 1916. It had cost half a million Allied casualties, mainly British, and cost the Turks at least a quarter of a million. In this period of the war there were further setbacks for the British, as when an expedition to Baghdad, an epic of inefficiency, was stopped in the winter of 1915–16 and a British division surrendered at Kut-el-Amara in the spring. Ottoman intervention, as far as the Germans were concerned, was now working out tolerably well.

But the Germans had done well elsewhere, too, mainly because the blockade had given them the will and the way for a proper war economy, ahead of others. The new commander (in effect: in this war, imperial figures were the nominal commanders-in-chief, and chiefs of staff were the real ones, much as generals pranced around on horses in public but used motor-cars if they had anything serious to do), Erich von Falkenhayn, was a much more calculating man than Moltke. He had a sense (perhaps exemplifying Goethe's famous line, 'genius knows when to stop') that taking on three Great Powers was beyond Germany's strength, and he told the Kaiser that if she did not lose this war she would in effect have won. His hope, and it dictated his doings, was that Russia could be persuaded to drop out and resume the partnership with Prussia that had reigned in much of the nineteenth century. He was a Bismarckian, not wishing, as Bismarck had said, 'to tie the trim Prussian frigate to a worm-eaten Austrian galleon', and he did not like the Austro-Hungarians, in his view frivolous Catholics with fancy manners (there was only one Catholic officer in the Prussian Guard – Franz von Papen, who ineptly organized sabotage of the American economy when he

was military attaché in Washington, and whose subsequent claim to fame is that he in effect appointed
Hitler). Like Bismarck, Falkenhayn thought that Germany should never part company with Russia, and his
relations with Conrad became, at times, frigid, to the
point where he simply did not reveal major decisions that
affected Austria-Hungary very greatly. At an important
stage he even got his liaison officer to find out by stealth
what the railway capacity north of Cracow was, so as to
stage an offensive about which he told his allies only a
week beforehand. At an even more vital point, he and
Conrad quite separately planned grand, supposedly
war-winning, attacks on France and Italy in complete
isolation from each other.

German peace-feelers towards Russia were left more
or less ignored, though the brightest retired Tsarist
statesmen would have taken up the offer. The western
Powers had offered the Tsar Constantinople, which
Falkenhayn could not do, and in any case there was
a campaign, somewhat vicious, against the substantial
German element in Russia, much of which dated back
to the days of Catherine the Great, who had brought in
German peasants to show the Russians how to practise
agriculture. Land reform – land to the peasant – had
been a great theme in Russian politics before 1914 and
now, if you were a war hero, there were provisions for
you to get confiscated German land. The Tsar's German
wife became a liability. At any rate, the Tsar was in no
position to discuss peace terms with the Germans, unless,
in effect, he had no choice.

Therefore, German attacks in the east. Falkenhayn, like Churchill, knew that the west offered only stalemate, and he was quite right. He tried one final attack in the west, again at Ypres in April 1915, and it was, like unrestricted U-Boat warfare, another exercise in Prussian crassness. A new weapon had come to hand – poison gas, banned by The Hague conventions, but justified for the weaseling reason that French rifle-bullets also released a gas on impact. It was indeed a horrible weapon, coming to blind or wreck the lungs of its victims. It was first tried out on the Russian front, in January, but the extreme cold reduced its effectiveness. In April, gas was released from cylinders, and it did cause immediate panic among the British and Canadians. But then the Germans themselves had to advance into it, and makeshift answers were found – cotton wool soaked in urine held off the effects for half an hour, and, later, there were proper gas masks. In any case, although the Ypres salient became even more uncomfortable for the British, there was no breakthrough, and Falkenhayn would not have known what to do with one. His main aim was at Russia.

Here, Falkenhayn had some good fortune, because the western Powers dispersed their effort between Gallipoli and the front in France. The latter caused fixation. On the map, the German line looked very vulnerable, because it bellied out in an extended salient, with Noyon, fifty miles from Paris, at the apex, and the French newspapers led every day with that news. Generals looking for favourable publicity were duly mesmerized: some new attack would bring about liberation of the national territory. British volunteers, in millions, had abandoned the boredom of life in industrial towns for the supposed glamour of a soldier's existence and were ready and willing to go. Salients were vulnerable to attacks from the sides, Artois on the northern edge, where the British Expeditionary Force was building up its strength, and Champagne, north-east of Paris, on the southern edge. If the British and French could break through in either area, then they could 'pour' cavalry through the gap, and perhaps surround the Germans in the central part of this salient. Here was the stuff of fantasy, and elderly generals, their experiences formed from cavalry charges in the South African veldt or the sand-table campaigns of Morocco, dreamt of glory. How this appeared on the ground has been described in one of the classic memoirs of the war, Robert Graves's *Goodbye to All That*. Graves was a public schoolboy, infused with the romantic patriotism of the time, and volunteered as he left Charterhouse. His regiment's regular officers believed in rituals. Officers dressed in baggy shorts, as if they were in India; colonels made it their business to make life humiliating for 'warts' – subalterns – even if, in civilian life, these had been prosperous and successful men. Not many of the commanders were at all bright, and some were downright dim.

The first attempt of the British Expeditionary Force had been at a village called Neuve Chapelle on 10 April. In this early stage of the war, trench-lines were still fairly undeveloped, and the British had massed guns in adequate numbers for the enemy trench to be overcome and then occupied. However, what then? German reserves arrived by train to another line, and British reserves came up on foot, each carrying sixty pounds of equipment – the equivalent of a heavy suitcase. The cavalry moved forward in expectation, and clogged the roads. But the guns had not registered the new German line, and the infantry were tired. Subsequent attacks therefore failed. These episodes were repeated in May, without the initial success. However, volunteers for the army were now arriving in droves, and in September, in concert with the French, a new and much more sizeable attack was planned. At Loos, a mining town, the British even released gas, but, as Graves describes the effort, it was a fiasco – the sort of British blunder that soldiers remember from the early stages of either world war. Gas was to be released from cylinders. The spanners to unscrew them were the wrong size. The chemistry teachers knew nothing much about poison gas, and hated what they were doing, and the military were not more respectful of bewildered chemistry teachers. The wind was wrong, but since the cylinders were in place, the order was given for the gas to be released, and it blew back on the British. The little town of Loos was captured, but the two reserve divisions were kept too far back, and advanced in a hurry over duck-boards in communications trenches, or along roads that were jammed axle-to-axle with carts, guns and the ineffable cavalry, arriving far too late to do anything further except be slaughtered over the next two days. This at least caused a change in the British command, because Sir John French was discredited and was replaced by Sir Douglas Haig, who had the king's ear and had performed quite creditably in 1914. The French attack in Champagne was rather more effective, in that on 25 September a sizeable artillery superiority, and then inefficient German defences, allowed a breakthrough and the capture, even, of 200 guns, a considerable haul. Reserves marched forward to exploit the gap, but then the problems re-asserted themselves – German defenders arriving by train, a new line to be reconnoitred and, a problem subsequently to become very well known, a battlefield to be crossed that had already been shattered by shelling, with shell-holes sometimes full of rain-water and corpses. The life-blood of France was draining away.

The life-blood of the Habsburg empire was also draining away, though with hundreds of thousands of captives rather than battle casualties. As 1915 began, the army was strung along the Carpathian mountains, hoping to hold the various passes. However, the fortress of Przemysl had been left behind in the retreat, and it contained 120,000 men, with supplies that would only last until the end of March. If circumstances had been as elsewhere, the place would no doubt have fallen to heavy guns, as Liège and the others did, but the Russian siege army had few. So, fatally, 'the bulwark on the San' (as propaganda called it) held out, and Austro-Hungarian prestige seemed to depend on it – if it did collapse, so, too, might military morale, and perhaps various potential enemies might be encouraged to inter-vene. However, it is an elementary mistake in strategy to become dependent on fortifications: the enemy thereby knows what you will have to do. Now, the Russians knew perfectly well that there would be Austrian relief attempts from the Carpathians; there was even a modest German force, *Südarmee*. From 23 January to the middle of March three of these attacks went ahead, at mountain altitudes, and even the Austrian official historians, whose kindness to Conrad sometimes involves suppression of truth, call it 'a cruel folly'. Whole units froze to death, shells either became buried in snow or bounced off ice, rifles had to be held over a fire before they would work. Some 800,000 men were sacrificed in these affairs, three quarters of them through sickness, and desertion became a serious problem. There were fears that many Slav troops, Ruthenes (Austrian Ukrainians) or Czechs in particular, would be unreliable, and one historic Prague regiment was even disbanded.

The Germans on their side were rather more suc-cessful. Hindenburg had taken the title 'Supreme Commander in the East' (shortened to *Oberost*) in Nov-ember, his forces having doubled in number from the twenty divisions at the start, and there were now tussles between Ludendorff and Falkenhayn, who resented his popularity and thought his plans far too ambitious. However, the Austro-Hungarian emergency did force Falkenhayn to send four newly formed army corps to the Russian front, and, early in February, these attacked south-east from the Prussian border, in an affair called 'the Winter Battle in Masuria'. In deep snow, the virtuosity of the German army was displayed, one Russian army being struck as it was forming up for an offensive, and another being taken so far by surprise that its commander, a man of seventy, had a nervous collapse and fled to the fortress of Kovno (he was sentenced to fifteen years' hard labour). One Russian army corps was trapped in a forest, as at Tannenberg on a smaller scale. After that, attacks were exchanged on the Polish–East Prussian borders, and they tended to show that Falkenhayn was right, that Ludendorff was too ambitious: unless there were spectacular Russian blundering, German losses were too high for any gains that might emerge. In any case, Austria-Hungary now needed direct assistance. On 22 March, Przemysl surrendered, and the Russian force thus freed was used for an attack across the Carpathian passes, leading towards the great plain of Hungary, and there were fears even for Budapest. Early in April, on Easter Sunday, a German force, the *Beskidenkorps*, under one of their most competent generals, Georg von der Marwitz, had staved off the immediate danger, but matters could clearly only become worse if nothing more substantial were done.

There was also a looming danger that everyone regarded as mortal: the likelihood of the intervention of Italy. How could Austria-Hungary take on a third front, and maybe even, if Romania came in as well, a fourth? Both were new states, their national unifications not completed, since the Habsburg empire had substantial Italian and Romanian populations. The Italians went one better, and looked at South Slav lands over the Adriatic, an empire in the Mediterranean at Turkey's expense, as well as a cheap loan of £50,000,000. They greatly feared Germany, but the Austro-Hungarian emergency and the Allied landing at Gallipoli made up for this, and Italy, on 26 April, signed a Treaty of London with the Allies, guaranteeing intervention. A decision for war was pushed through a parliament that was not widely enthusiastic, and on 23 May the Italian ambassador in Vienna handed it over. In theory this should have been the end of Austria, but geography greatly helped. Most of the Austro-Italian border was very mountainous, and there was only about twenty miles of flat land, north-west of the great port of Trieste which was the Italians' main objective. However, it was *karst*, flintstone, in which nothing grew and trenches could not be dug. Even the scratch forces that the Austrians put up managed to hold the initial attacks. Far from destroying Austria-Hungary, Italian intervention gave the war some point as far as many Slavs were concerned, and the Prague regiment was, in due course, reconstituted because its men gave a very good account of themselves on the Italian front. Besides, Italian intervention led Falkenhayn into one of the greatest successes of the war, in the east.

Falkenhayn had had two main concerns. The first was to persuade Russia to abandon the war, and he needed some demonstration that she would never win it. The second was to persuade the Austro-Hungarians that they should make generous concessions to Italy, so as to fend off her intervention. This was difficult; if he told them that he proposed to send direct help, with a view to defeating Russia, then he might encourage them to refuse the Italian concessions. The preparations for an attack on Russia were therefore concealed even from Conrad, and the Kaiser himself was only told of the plan on 11 April. It was a good plan – an attack by a new army (the Eleventh) across rolling countryside north of the Carpathians, in the passes of which the Russians were attempting offensives. By now the land had dried out, and there would be no repetition of the calamitous Conrad doings in the snows. Over ten days, the eight divisions – 100,000 men and 1,000 guns – of Macken-sen's new Eleventh Army arrived east of Cracow by the end of April – the kind of railway performance of which Russians, especially, were not capable.

They arrived at a very sensitive spot, an area where the Russians' difficulties with war goods were compounded by a very messy strategic situation: their entire position was about to explode. The Russian army consisted of two Army Groups (or *fronty*). The North-western one had to deal with the Germans in East Prussia, who could attack south, east, even north, into the Baltic provinces. A cautious commander would have to keep men ready to defend any of these, which left nothing spare for an attack. The South-western *front* equally naturally worried about threats to the long Carpathian flank, and in any case thought, understand-ably, that a certain effort would put Austria-Hungary out of the war. The problem on the Russian side

especially was that the troops' movements were extraordinarily slow, because their railway system was considerably less advanced than the German, and there was
almost no central railway direction beyond a middle-
ranking officer with two assistants sitting in half of a
railway carriage in a forest clearing at Baranowicze.
About one fifth of German railway movement was to do
with horses (especially fodder), but more than one half
on the Russian side, partly because cavalry and Cossacks
were still expecting their hour of glory. But in any case,
the *fronty* managed their own railway movements,
ignored *Stavka*, and did not put each other's claims first.
It could take a month for an army corps to be shifted,
although in theory the journey from Riga to Odessa
could have been done in five days.

Two thirds of the entire strength, sixty divisions,
catered for North-western phobias about East Prussia.
The commander of the South-western Army Group
(Ivanov) was assembling a large force (six army corps)
for an action close to the Romanian border, in the
eastern Carpathians – the aim, of course, to bring in
Romania and Italy at the same time. Most Russian
troops to the west of this were supposed to keep on in
the Carpathian passes, and the result was that the front
east of Cracow was thinly held, by five divisions, with
no reserves within easy reach, and a sketchy front line,
some desultory earth-shifting and not much wire. Russian soldiers disliked digging in ground that had been
fought over, because, in the thaw, corpses surfaced. The
local commander heard that German troops were

arriving, and wanted to build a reserve position. He was told that, if he had men to spare for that sort of work, he must have more than he needed, and was told to part with some. Communications to the front line even ran over open ground. Everything, strategic and tactical, was in place for one of the great disasters of Russian military history.

On 2 May the eighteen divisions and thousand guns of the Austrian Fourth and German Eleventh Armies began a bombardment lasting four hours, which quite soon reduced the Russian positions to rubble and could not be answered, most of the Russian Third Army's artillery being elsewhere (and even the commander, though forewarned by deserters, had gone off to a celebration of the St George Order). Many of the troops were raw or even over-age, and some panicked at the trench mortars, running away, greatcoats flapping, over open ground; one third of the defenders were wiped out, and a gap of five miles opened in the Russian line. In two days the Central Powers' troops moved eight miles. Only an immediate Russian retreat to the river San and Przemysl might have saved something, but the Third Army was ordered to hold on, local reserves vanished into the defeat, and by 10 May the Austro-Germans had taken 200 guns and 140,000 prisoners. Now, the Russians had to pull back from the Carpathians, and reserves from the other *front* were sent tardily, reluctantly, and in bits and pieces. Besides, another sinister factor was starting to tell: the Russians did not have sufficient munitions – one corps, needing 20,000 shells at once and 25,000 every day thereafter, could only be sent 15,000. By 19 May the Germans had a bridgehead over the San, and when Falkenhayn met the chief of staff of the Eleventh Army, Hans von Seeckt, at Jaroslaw on the river, the two men agreed that an enormous opportunity was opening up: the whole of Russian Poland might be taken. The commander of the Russian South-west *front* agreed, sending panic-stricken messages that he would have to retreat as far as Kiev. Meanwhile, he had to retreat eccentrically – between north and east, not quite knowing which route the Central Powers would follow. On 4 June Przemysl was re-taken, and on the 22nd Lvov itself.

There followed a vast crisis on the Russian front. The great battering-ram in Galicia now moved towards the southern side of Russian Poland, and in mid July the Germans in East Prussia assembled another battering-ram for the northern side. There was a further complication, in that the Germans had opened another front, on the Baltic. In mid April they had sent cavalry into the open spaces there, and had drawn in more Russian troops than the area was worth; an Army had to cover Riga, another Lithuania, and a new *front*, the Northern, was opened up, giving the usual headaches as to the disposal of reserves. The Russian strategic position was a very poor one, and the sensible thing would have been to give up Poland altogether. However, the rare voice to that effect was easily silenced. In the first place, evacuating Warsaw would require 2,000 trains, and these could not be spared because of the requirements of fodder.

There was another argument. Poland was supposed to be protected by the great fortresses – Kovno in the north, Novogeorgievsk outside Warsaw, the very symbol of Russian rule, and lesser ones elsewhere, on various rivers. These fortresses had been very expensive before the war, and contained thousands of guns, with millions of rounds of shell. Why just abandon them?

The Russian army would therefore stand and fight. Shell-shortage had been brought about, not really by the terrible backwardness of the country (as Stalin and emigrant generals, all seeking excuses for their misdeeds, asserted) but by wrong-headedness. The War Ministry had never thought Russian industrialists honest or competent. The Artillery Department of the Ministry thought that the infantry were producing hard-luck stories. Foreigners were invited to supply shell, but Russia came at the end of everyone's list, sent specifications in measurements as obsolete as the cubit, and anyway could not directly pay (she used British credit). But the fact remains that two million shells had been stockpiled in the great fortresses, which now collapsed. In mid July, Gallwitz, with a thousand guns and 400,000 shells from the north, and Mackensen from the south, bombarded their way forward, sometimes reducing Russian army corps to a few thousand men, and by 4 August the Germans had taken Warsaw. The fortress of Novogeorgievsk had a large garrison, with 1,600 guns and a million shells. It should have been evacuated, given the fate of every other fortress in Europe faced with heavy artillery, but as the *front* commander, Alexeyev, opined, 'spiritual motives speak for its defence'. Beseler, conqueror of the fortress of Antwerp, arrived with a siege train. He captured the chief engineer of the fortress, doing the rounds with all of his maps. A single German shell blew up one of the forts, and the place surrendered on 19 August. At the same moment, the same fate occurred to the other great fortress, Kovno, which was supposed to defend Lithuania, and where there was a similar vast haul of 1,300 guns and 900,000 shells.

As the Turkish proverb has it, one disaster is worth a thousand pieces of advice, and *Stavka* at last did the right thing. It retreated – a version of 1812, complete with scorched-earth tactics, leaving nothing behind for the Germans to use. From the military viewpoint, the retreat was managed well enough, Brest-Litovsk being burned, with hundreds of thousands of refugees trudging away from the Jewish Pale and crowding into the cities. The Germans outran their own supplies, even of water, as they plodded ahead into the marshlands of the Pripyat. Because *Stavka* overrated the German threat to Riga, the retreat proceeded in different directions. On 18 September the Germans stole through the 'Sventsiany gap' and managed to take Vilna, capital of Lithuania. Ludendorff wanted to go on, but Falkenhayn had some sense of reality. The Russians had lost a million prisoners, and would clearly be in no position to interfere with German plans elsewhere; in any case, as a technician, Falkenhayn well understood the difficulties of supplying armies in White Russia, far beyond the German rail-heads, without metalled roads, and dependent on a barely functioning Russian railway that had a broader gauge unusable by German locomotives. A priority now was to knock out Serbia and to establish a land route to Turkey, before the Balkan winter set in. He waved aside Austro-Hungarian plans concerning the Ukraine and Italy, and sent Mackensen to the Balkans. The Bulgarian government had their own ambitions, to reconstitute the medieval Bulgarian empire, and Bulgaria was strategically placed to invade Serbia from the east. She was overwhelmed in October–November, and on 1 January 1916, the first direct train from Berlin arrived in Istanbul.

NOTES

1. A Colonel Doughty-Wylie, on the Staff, went ashore armed with only a cane. He had been Military Consul (part of an early international effort at peace-keeping in south-eastern Anatolia), had taken part, with the Red Crescent, in the Balkan Wars on the Ottoman side, and been decorated. He said that he was not going to kill Turks, was himself killed, and was awarded a posthumous Victoria Cross.

WWI

preceding pages: British gasmasked machine-gun unit on the Somme, 1916

In December 1915 the Allies held a military conference at French General Headquarters, in the palace of the Princes de Condé, at Chantilly. The year had gone badly for them. However, 1916 promised much better: the Russians had overcome their munitions crisis, and the British were producing a land army; they were also financing the imports (mainly from the USA) which were so vital for the Allied war effort. Falkenhayn could tell that time was not on Germany's side. He could also see that Britain was the key enemy: she would fight on, unless somehow France could be made to ask for peace. Germany still had an advantage in terms of munitions-output, so the obvious target was the French army, and the obvious method was artillery – competently used, it caused three quarters of all casualties. The German superiority in it was still substantial, and it needed to be used in a place where the French would have no alternative but to stand and be battered. That in turn was obvious – Verdun. Here was a historic place, a fortress dominating the heights of the Meuse, north-east of Paris, which had acted as hinge of the French army in the Battle of the Marne and had a place in the mythology of France greater than that of Ypres in the mythology of England. It would have to be defended, though its defenders, given the terrain, could be shelled to pieces.

Such was Falkenhayn's thinking, and in some ways it made sense. There was a German salient at St Mihiel, to the south, from which Verdun's communications could be bombarded, and if he took the heights east of the river, his guns could bombard Verdun itself. German communications were much better than the defenders', which consisted mainly of a single winding and uphill road. Besides, the winter mists and the forests meant that an attack could gain surprise, and air superiority had been attained. The French would have to counter-attack in exceedingly unfavourable circumstances, had already suffered greatly during Joffre's doings in 1915, and would be bled to death. The Fifth Army was placed under the command of the Crown Prince, with a von der Schulenburg, from one of the historic Prussian military dynasties, as chief of staff, and matters began as Falken-hayn had foreseen. Verdun had been quiet, and French positions had not been properly prepared. Inspection in January created some alarm, and the generals would probably just have abandoned the position, but the politicians supervened, and said that the glory of France forbade withdrawal. The Crown Prince needed to muster only nine divisions, because the essentials lay with the artillery – 1,300 munitions trains in seven weeks. There was a delay, caused by weather conditions, and this allowed French preparations to be intensified – perhaps decisively. On 21 February 1,220 guns, half of them heavy or high-trajectory, fired off two million shells in eight hours on an eight-mile front. In the first three days, the Germans advanced several miles, with new tactics and new weaponry, such as flamethrowers. The symbol of the battle was a great fort, Douaumont, which the French had had the sense to abandon (its concrete was extremely thick, but of course it made an obvious target for the heaviest of guns, though, after its capture, it was a French gun that smashed it). The Germans took it in a lucky probe, the French having opted to use trenches outside it.

But Falkenhayn's ideas were defective. Two million shells could of course obliterate anything living on an eight-mile front, but the front was not long enough to deal with the French on the west bank of the Meuse, and they fired at the flank of the Germans advancing on the right bank. The defending commander, Philippe Pétain, knew what he was about, and German momentum slowed. Falkenhayn had to try and deal with the left bank problem, and in the meantime on the right bank had to fend off suicidal counter-attacking by a general determined to make his name, Nivelle. The French did not collapse – quite the contrary – and the decisive heights east of the Meuse, after Douaumont, were not taken. Meanwhile, Verdun became transformed into a national epic, something like the Battle of Britain in 1940, and France was galvanized. Public opinion was whipped up on both sides, and Falkenhayn's limited aims were forgotten.

Three quarters of a million casualties ensued, French and German. The single road, the 'sacred way' as it was rather blasphemously named, was improvised, and lorries went by every fourteen seconds, at night, their lights dimmed, to supply the Verdun line. French divisions were rotated, almost all of them spending two weeks at least in line. Falkenhayn realized that he would have to silence the artillery on the western bank of the Meuse, and in March and April he concentrated his efforts there. He himself would probably have preferred to break off the operation, but it had become a matter of prestige, the Kaiser himself visiting to celebrate the fall of Fort Douaumont, and urging on his son. The Germans did capture two of the western heights – Mort Homme and Côte 304 – and then turned their attention to the east bank again, in May and June, taking Fort Vaux, but this had not been the point of the exercise at all – it had been the French who were supposed to do the attacking. To begin with, French losses had been much greater than German, but now the figures were equalized. When on 23 June the final great German effort came, it was too weak to prevail. Thereafter, the energetic new commander, General Nivelle, organized well-planned counter-strokes, re-taking the forts (there is a scene in Renoir's great film *La Grande illusion* when the French prisoners of war go mad, shouting '*Douaumont est à nous*'). Verdun also gave France a slogan, '*ils ne passeront pas*'. But in a sense it broke the French army, or at any rate strained it to such a degree that the country never really recovered: France's last moment as a Great Power. When she did fall in 1940, this was partly because her people did not want to go through Verdun again.

Perhaps, if Falkenhayn had helped the Austrians, Italy might have been knocked out of the war, and that was the Austrian aim. In mid May, the Austrians attacked from the Trentino, hoping to break out onto the Venetian plain, and even cut off the whole Italian army on the Isonzo, north-east of Venice. It was a very bold plan, and in weather that was still wintry the Austrians performed prodigies, hauling heavy guns with ski-lift cable cars. This gave them a threefold advantage in heavy artillery, and by shifting six of his best divisions from the eastern front, Conrad gained a slight superiority. Within days the Austrians were near the edge of the plateau, but as usual the defenders' communications were better, while the attackers were exhausted; reserves came up by Fiat lorries, for counter-attack. This was the only real might-have-been in the war. If Falkenhayn had supported Conrad, then Italy could easily have been knocked out altogether, with dramatic consequences for the other fronts. The option was never seriously considered; Falkenhayn did not even tell Conrad about his plans, nor did Conrad tell Falkenhayn: the two men were on very bad terms.

There was one decisive battle on the Russian front – decisive in the sense that it deprived most Russian generals of their stomachs. They had to do something, according to the Chantilly agreements, to assist the French over Verdun. On 18 March, in White Russia,

near Lake Narotch, the northern Russian armies therefore began an offensive, reckoning, with some justification, that earlier supply problems had been overcome. It
was a copy-book example of how not to do things.
The troops were marched over snow, easily spotted by
German aircraft; even the cooks in headquarters were
discussing when the offensive would take place. The
thaw had begun: icy mud during the day, frozen mud
during the night, which meant that shell was either
swamped or it bounced off. On top of everything else,
there was a row between light artillerists and heavy artillerists, with no cooperation, and the initial bombardment was ineffective, dismissed as 'General Smirnov's
son et lumière'. After 100,000 casualties and no gains,
the attack was called off – probably, and with considerable competition, the worst-managed battle of the entire
war. Educated Russia was starting to look on the Tsarist
establishment with derision. The press department of
Stavka was run by a Mikhail Lemke, the translator of
Hegel, and his diaries, published in 1918, are a record
of mockery – General Smirnov, far too old, appointed
because some painted old granny had intrigued at the
court, General Bezobrazov, pop-eyed and log-legged,
even worse. General Kuropatkin thought up a wheeze
by which, in the middle of the night, searchlights would
suddenly be switched on, supposedly to dazzle the
Germans. It had not occurred to him that the attackers
would be silhouetted and be easy targets. He was dismissed. However, the Tsar, to spare his feelings, did not
want him to think that he had been sacked for being too

old; he was kindly told that he had just been incompetent, and was replaced by someone even older. Lemke titters in disbelief, but a much greater disaffection was under way. After Lake Narotch, the Russian northern armies did next to nothing for a full year and a half – bored, badly fed, drinking on empty stomachs foul stuff brewed in secret: the very prescription for a mutiny, which was duly to happen on an enormous scale.

There was a further non-battle at this time, decisive in much the same way. The Tirpitz navy and the British Grand Fleet had become book-ends, one in Wilhelmshaven and the other in Scapa Flow, at the northern edge of Scotland, both more or less immobilized by threats of mines and submarines. Before the war, that this would happen had been clear enough, and the British had tried to drill it into German heads: both sides wasted enormous amounts of money on ships that would never do anything. On 31 May, in the context of Verdun, the Germans sailed forth, the intention being to destroy the fast British battle-cruisers, which deterred attacks on the cross-Channel troop-traffic or the sending of commerce raiders into the wider ocean. Through intelligence work, the British were not taken by surprise. The two fleets had to move with much caution, for fear of mines and torpedoes, and since the newest British battleships had powerful turbines and had enormous guns, the range was such that the ships hardly even needed to see each other (though the accuracy of shooting was low, and most rounds missed). In a sense this was the same story as on the Western Front – enormous weight but a hopelessly limited capacity of control. The British were dependent on old-fashioned signal flags: it was difficult simply to know what was going on, and the British commander, Jellicoe, behaved with great caution, knowing that, if an action went wrong, he could lose the war in an afternoon. This battle of Jutland lasted only a few hours, with 150 ships on the British side, 100 on the German. Losses were 14 to 11, before the Germans prudently retired. They had obviously had the better of the day, British ships being less well armoured and having fewer watertight bulkheads: but the Germans reckoned that they had had a narrow escape, and that there was no way of eliminating the British naval superiority by fleet action. Their Admiralty now proposed submarines instead, and the High Seas Fleet remained in port, indeed becoming a 'risk fleet' in the sense that the German empire itself was at risk, realized two and a half years later, of being overthrown by the resentful and drunken sailors.

The British had not expected to have to produce a land army, and at first the authorities had been overwhelmed by the great numbers of men who volunteered. However, they were now in a position to do something with their 'New Arm' (as it was called) and the French emergency gave some urgency to this. Chantilly had agreed that there was to be a Franco-British effort, the French, originally, to have taken the lead. The new British commander, Douglas Haig, would have preferred an attack in Flanders, which might at least clear the Belgian coast, but the simple fact was that the French and British armies adjoined around Amiens, the chief place in Picardy, astride the river Somme – an area where poppies grow in profusion. They have become the symbol of the British war dead.

There was no particular strategic significance for an attack on the Somme. True, Haig still imagined that the German line could be breached and cavalry could pour through the gap, but it could have been poured more effectively elsewhere, in so far as it could be poured at all. As the German line solidified in 1914, it had done so along ridges, not substantial in absolute terms but certainly substantial in relative terms, which allowed their guns a greater advantage, and also gave them the benefit of earth less likely to turn into mud, because further from the water-table. The most that Haig could do would be to take those ridges. However, the British war industry was now able to make thousands of guns and millions of shells and so, as in other armies, the general idea was to launch an enormous bombardment, with an attack on twenty miles of front (long enough for the advancing troops not to be enfiladed).

Haig did not trust his men's capacity, and therefore relied on crushing bombardment. True, for any pre-war soldier, the quantities of matériel available seemed enormous, but that was not really the case, given the scale of the task. There were other problems – firstly that a considerable number of the shells were 'duds' or fell short, and secondly that the artillery were not adequately trained for their task. One war-winner was the 'creeping barrage', a curtain of fire that advanced steadily some fifty yards ahead of the infantry, forcing the defenders to keep their heads well and truly down. However, that meant a degree of communication and control quite beyond the British army's capacity at this time. Telephone and radio were liable to break down, carrier pigeons were inadequate, and the barrage had to be directed by an observation officer, perched, a very obvious target, in a tree or on a tall building. But the army's learning curve was in any case still in its early stages. Haig's artillery expert was moved in at the last minute, expected to share his office with two other men, and allowed no reference manuals, let alone any of the foreign literature on the subject. The British manual gave the game away when it grandly stated that 'accuracy is a new demand in this war'. But the infantry themselves were also hardly trained, and (as with the French in 1914) were expected only to perform the simplest of tactics – advancing in rigid long lines, officers striding out front. A final problem lay with the ministry of munitions: it still produced shrapnel, which exploded in the air above a defensive position, scattering projectiles, maybe useful for cutting barbed wire but not against the deep dug-outs that the Germans were now constructing as a matter of course. There was not enough high-explosive shell, which exploded on or just after impact (special fuses could delay the explosion for some seconds as the shell buried itself, which did real damage to barbed wire). A further problem was amateurishness in managing trains: a jam, eighteen miles long, between Amiens and Abbeville, was not sorted out until the usual peppery Scotsman arrived and sacked everyone responsible.

The British bombardment began on 24 June, just as the last German effort at Verdun was ebbing away, and went on for a week: the expectation being that everything would be wrecked. But 400 heavy guns and 1,000 field guns were not enough to deal with a defensive system of three miles' depth and twenty miles' length. The fact of its start gave the Germans ample warning of an attack, and it churned the front line into mud that was often quite impassable. The Germans on their ridges had dug very deeply, lining the defences with concrete, and these systems were not knocked out at all: the artillery was still active, and there were lines of machine guns to deal with the 'waves' of infantry that emerged from the British trenches on 1 July, the officers sometimes kicking footballs to inspire confidence. The names on the war memorials of Eton and Oxford and Cambridge and Edinburgh go on and on (to the credit of New College, Oxford, and Trinity, Cambridge, they include German and Hungarian names). On that day, there were 20,000 British dead, the worst disaster in the whole of British military history. There were 37,000 other casualties, and there was almost no gain at all – on the right, at Mametz, a section of the German front line was taken, but elsewhere, nothing. The French, to the south-east, overran the entire front line and advanced towards the second line, but they employed many more guns per mile of front, and their tactics had been learned in the hard school of Verdun.

The fact was that breakthrough, as imagined by Haig, was not possible, short of utterly crushing artillery weight, and even then there were severe limits. Between early July and November, necessity sometimes imposed itself on Haig, and when it did he confined himself to well-prepared local actions, with a very limited objective. Accordingly, there were small successes now and then. Thus in mid July there was a well-managed advance on a limited front by the South Africans, but then cavalry came up and got nowhere. In the first phase, in July and August, there were narrow-front, uncoordinated oper-ations attracting enemy gunnery – losses higher than on the first day, and not much more to show for it. There was, it is true, much worry on the German side, because of the strength of British artillery – seven million shells were fired between 2 July and mid September, and German regimental histories reveal the strain of this *Materialschlacht*. In the middle period of the battle, the Germans were ordered to regain every piece of ground lost, regardless of its tactical value. In this way the defence was costlier to the Germans than it needed to be.

By mid September Haig was prepared for a new effort, and one involving a new weapon, the tank. It was spec-tacular enough – a monster of metal, moving on cater-pillar tracks and immune from small-arms fire; many inventors claimed credit for it, and H. G. Wells had imagined it. 'Tank' had been its code-name when ex-periments went ahead – in the Admiralty, thanks to

Churchill, rather than in the War Office, which had other things on its mind (as did its German equivalent). Tanks developed a certain mythology, but they had their limits. The internal combustion engine had not really developed far enough to take thirty tons of weight, and the tanks easily broke down; they also moved very slowly, and, though the armour was thick, they could be put out of action by a well-aimed shell. In effect, they needed to be combined with other arms, aircraft and infantry. But the real queen of the battlefield remained artillery, and here the British were learning: they understood the importance of the 'creeping barrage'. In mid September, not seeing how tanks and infantry might cooperate, Haig did not use it, fearing that tanks would be hit, and in their first appearance on the battlefield, tanks did not flourish, while, as ever, cavalry clogged the rear areas, waiting for a breakthrough that never came. But then, in the latter part of September, the creeping bombardment was adopted and part of the German front line was taken. It no longer mattered much, except in the sense that episodes such as this – modest successes – caused Haig to think that he might gain a great victory if only he kept on. And he kept on, and on: the Somme petering out only in November, in mud and rain. The justification advanced for the whole business was that it had damaged German morale, and the official historians took Haig's part, even pronouncing that 600,000 Germans had been knocked out, as against 400,000 British and French – a reversal of the usual pattern of losses in an offensive. C. S. Forrester wrote a novel, *The General*, in an attempt to understand the senior military mind that had made such affairs possible. He remarked that the western-front generals were trying to hammer in a screw and, when it resisted, trying to hammer it harder. Necessity in the event showed how such battles should be fought, but the learning process was long and bloody.

There was only one senior man in this period who had an early understanding of it – a Russian, A. A. Brusilov. He commanded the South-western *front* against the Austrians. After Lake Narotch, the other *front* commanders, elderly and nervous, had more or less given up hope: the Germans were unbeatable, they thought. Late in May, appeals came from Italy for some diversionary attack, and these generals shook their heads, on the grounds that their forces did not have the unimaginable amounts of heavy shell that they thought necessary. Brusilov caused still more head-shaking when he volunteered to attack. But he had thought things through.

The problem with this war was that various solutions ruled each other out. If you tried to break through, it meant bringing up an enormous number of men and great quantities of supplies: there would therefore be no surprise, and the huge initial bombardment would make this certain. The enemy would have reserves to hand. Now, sheer weight might indeed produce a break-through, in the sense that everything ahead would have been obliterated. The troops would then advance on foot. They would do so at about two miles per hour – less, if fired upon – because each man had to carry what he needed for survival, including an entrenching tool, water, and so on. Meanwhile, the enemy would be constructing a new line, bringing up reserves either by train or by lorry (or, in France, buses). There would be further attacks by tired men, supported by guns wearisomely hauled forward through the mud by teams of perhaps hungry horses and not registered for the new targets. The result would be as in the French Champagne offensive of September 1915, or the British effort on the Somme. The key therefore must be disruption of the enemy reserves. That would mean attacking in several places at once, so that the reserves would not know where to proceed. It would also mean a short bombardment. Each attack should be launched on a relatively wide front, so that local reserves, too, would be bewildered (and the problem of enfilading fire, as at Verdun, overcome). It was all very bold, and required well-trained troops and officers. Brusilov's headquarters stood out for their quality – not overburdened by ceremonial, orders short and to the point. His leadership qualities were shown in the care with which the troops managed the preparation – constructing huge underground hiding places, the guns registering unobtrusively. Brusilov had four separate armies and each was to attack.

On the Austro-Hungarian side, all was serenity: Archduke Joseph Ferdinand, commanding the Fourth Army in the northern part of the line, enjoyed himself boating on the river Styr with his cronies, and talked of 'our formidable positions' (some of the dug-outs even had glass windows). Surprise was almost total when, on

4 June, Brusilov's northernmost army began, with a four-hour bombardment. The weather had dried out the Austrian positions, and they crumbled quickly, releasing a huge cloud of dust, which hid the attacking Russians. Austrian local reserves were thrown in, and vanished; troops, cut off, gave up all too easily, and Brusilov had also worked out sensible tactics against such strong points as held out – he simply ignored them, pushing his men forward as far as they could go, to disrupt the enemy command system. By the end of the day, the Austrian Fourth Army was near dissolution – a telegram went off to Vienna saying that it 'has been captured'. In this situation, reserves should have arrived to seal off the gap. But here again Brusilov had found the answer, because his other armies also attacked. There was a further crisis far to the south, on the Romanian border, where the Austrian Seventh Army (commanded by a good general, Pflanzer-Baltin, and using Hungarian troops, whose loyalty was not in question) found that its retreat, on both sides of the river Pruth, led to muddle, and the central two Russian armies, though not doing as spectacularly as the others, also made respectable progress. Where were the defenders' reserves to go? They moved first towards the Fourth Army, then the order was countermanded, then it was reinstated – all of this on hot, dusty roads, or very slow-moving trains. In the event they were not thrown in at all, or were thrown in in little packets. Brusilov had advanced sixty miles along the front, and took 350,000 prisoners. Hardly surprisingly, the morale of Austria-Hungary's Czech and

Ruthene soldiery now did indeed make for problems, and it would need stiffening from ruthless Prussian NCOs for them to be overcome. There were demands, now, for an incorporation of the Austro-Hungarian army into the German, as the price for survival, and soon thereafter Hindenburg and Ludendorff were effectively its commanders. The mixing of troops sometimes went down to battalion level, and it would have been very difficult for Austria-Hungary to withdraw from the war with a separate army.

But Brusilov had in any event missed out the final element of his winning formula: knowing when to stop. All of Russia was wild with enthusiasm, and the Allies expected great things. His men were therefore pushed forward, exhausting themselves in the summer heat and facing the usual supply problems, especially with regard to water, as the streams dried up. In the meantime, Austrian troops from the Italian front, and Germans taken from the northern side of the eastern front and even from the threatened western one, arrived and set up a new line close to the railway heads at Kovel and Vladimir Volynsk. Russian cavalry proved, as ever, ineffective, and fodder for it made the supply problem all the worse. Russian attacks were of diminishing effectiveness, and the bulk of Russia's reserves were on the German part of the line. The Russian generals there were prodded into offensive action, early in July, in the wooded area of Baranowicze, which in 1914 had been the site of the high command. The attack went more or less as other such attacks had gone – frontal charges, after an ineffective and wasteful bombardment – and the generals of course pointed to such results as an excuse for doing nothing further. The reserves were then sent south to Brusilov. The chief element was an entirely new 'Special Army', made up mainly of the Imperial Guard's two infantry and one cavalry corps – the best men in the old army. These were trained, not in modern warfare, but in tactics that would have suited the generation before, and the commander, Bezobrazov, was an elderly crony of the Tsar's, with corps commanders to match. From mid July, at fortnightly intervals, this Guard Army charged across the marshes around the town of Kovel, where a breakthrough might have cut a German lateral railway. Fighting, said the German general involved, von der Marwitz, had come to resemble conditions in the West, and Russian corpses heaped up. Bezobrazov asked for a truce to clear the bodies, and was refused: there could be no greater deterrent to future attacks. They petered out in August.

They did, however, bring in Romania. Her leaders had been nervous of intervention, knowing the fate of Serbia, but the Allies pressed hard, offering great rewards of Hungarian territory, and promising an attack from the southern Balkans (where, since 1915, they had had a base, at Salonica, partly garrisoned by what was left of the Serbian army). There was panic in Berlin and Vienna: Falkenhayn lost his office (and was sent to command the Ninth Army on the new front). But the Romanians had almost no experience of real war, and though the men were tough, the officers knew little, and their ways amazed observers (among the first orders was a prescription that junior officers were not to use eye-shadow). The army staggered over the Carpathian passes into Transylvania and then became involved in a supply snarl-up. Troops were somehow scraped together by the Central Powers, now that the Brusilov offensive had lost its momentum (Russia had incurred a million casualties). Skilled mountain-troops advanced into the passes. The Allies at Salonica faced not just problems of supply, but constant malaria, and the town itself suffered a great fire. A mixed German, Bulgarian and Turkish force was therefore free to attack northwards, over the Bulgarian Danube border. The Romanians vacillated as to which front should have priority, choosing first one, then the other, losing on both. By early November, the Central Powers were through the westernmost passes of the Transylvanian Alps, and they were over the Danube as well. The Romanian army, at risk of being cut off, evacuated the capital, Bucharest, on 7 December, and had to withdraw, under quarrelsome Russian protection, through the smoke of endless burning oil wells to a new defensive front in the mountains of Moldavia.

In 1916, the world of nineteenth-century Europe died – an appropriate symbol of this being the death of Franz Joseph, the old emperor of Austria, on 21 November. He had been born in 1830, just as the age of railways, of parliamentary liberalism, was starting; he had become the great-grandfather of the various peoples of his empire, all of whose languages he could speak. Now, in

1916, nationalism was sweeping all before it, and the masses were involved as never before, some of the media egging them on. The State was now required to take on far more than in 1913, printing paper money to pay for it all or putting up direct taxes to unheard-of levels. At the end of 1916 there was a further symbol, in London, of the old world's end: the old Liberal-dominated Coalition lost a parliamentary vote on whether enemy property in Nigeria could be confiscated. A few ultra-conservatives, appalled at the slaughter, wished for peace, but they no longer had any power: in all countries, even the experiences of 1916 only produced demands for 'war to a victorious conclusion', as the Russian slogan ran. A new British war leader emerged, David Lloyd George, and he wanted a 'knock-out blow'.

WWI

*preceding pages: Russian troops in eastern Galicia
running past a church during an unidentified
battle, 1917*

Great wars develop a momentum of their own. As German historians have pointed out, the statesmen in 1914 had thought in terms of a 'cabinet war', that is, one that could be turned on and off at the will of a few leaders. But with mass conscription, and the enormous loss of life and limb, sheer hatred of the enemy, and the emergence of a monster of public opinion that no politician could ignore, the war could not simply be ended with some recognition that it had all been a gigantic mistake. The Austrian emperor would have liked to do this; so would the Pope; so would President Wilson. They were waved aside, and at the turn of 1916 and 1917, radical leaders emerged, offering one or other version of Lloyd George's 'knock-out blow'. And a further twist in the tragedy was that, on each side, such a blow seemed entirely possible. The new leaders in Germany, Ludendorff especially, might recognize that in the west there was stalemate. But submarines, to starve the British out – why not? A few people on the Left did break with the Social Democrats, but there was no other serious opposition at this moment. On the contrary, the country became more militarized than ever before: a 'Hindenburg Programme' made every male from sixteen to sixty liable for war work, and output was expected to double (it did). In France, in parallel, the energetic new general, Robert Nivelle, who had made his reputation at Verdun, promised the great victory that had eluded old Joffre, who was now made Marshal of France and sidelined. There had been a miracle of improvisation as regards the war economy, despite the loss of the industrial *Nord*, and Nivelle promised confidently that he could win the war by mathematical methods, combining new infantry methods and carefully managed 'creeping barrages'.

But it was the Germans who first translated the new *jusqu'au boutiste* ('to the very end') mood into practice. They proclaimed unrestricted submarine warfare. This was a revolutionary business, because it brought the risk that the USA would enter the war on the Allied side. American trade with the British had vastly risen, and much of the economy depended upon it. The British had been by far the greatest foreign investors in the USA, and now these investments were being sold off to pay for the imports. What would happen if American trade were stopped by submarine sinkings, with the attendant drownings of civilians? The Americans did not, generally, have any desire at all to intervene, and their president, Woodrow Wilson, had called for a compromise peace. U-Boats might change that.

However, the new High Command in Germany were clear that there could be no victory in the west as matters stood, and they looked to the navy. The naval authorities, as a matter of professional pride, resented the inactivity of their great ships, but they had discovered how effective the submarine could be almost as soon as the war broke out, when *U-9* sank three British cruisers. If they could torpedo civilian ships supplying Great Britain, then the British ocean lifeline would be cut, and the British population would face the privation that Germans were undergoing in 'the turnip winter' of 1916–17. There were two great problems. The first was a formal one, that international law forbade the sinking, without warning, of civilian (and maybe neutral) ships. Common humanity said that people should have a chance to get to lifeboats, and in any case the ship might easily not be carrying war goods. Possibly, the USA would enter the war if American ships were sunk. These arguments were widely dismissed as *Humanitätsdüselei* – 'humanitarian babbling' – and in any case most Germans were by now convinced that the British were trying to starve them. They were also convinced, and not unfairly, that the USA had been quite disproportionately helpful to the Allies – banks giving credit that held up the international value of the British pound and trade, keeping the French war economy going. If the USA did intervene, would it really make any significant difference?

The second problem counted for more. The Germans did not, in 1915, have enough submarines – fifty-four, most carrying only four torpedoes, and short in range. They were supposed, on encountering a ship in British

waters, to surface, enquire what was on board, inspect
it and, where appropriate, allow the ship's company to
take to lifeboats before the ship was sunk. This proceeding – 'cruiser rules' – exposed a submarine to concealed
guns, but the alternative – sinking upon sight, a torpedo
gliding silently just below the waterline, against a ship
containing women and children – counted as barbaric,
inhuman (as Churchill had said in 1914: he could not
even imagine such methods being used). In the early
months of 1915, to counter the British blockade, 'unrestricted' submarine warfare – sink on sight – had been
declared, a forbidden zone being demarcated around the
British Isles, and the *Lusitania* passenger liner had been
sunk, on 7 May 1915, with due loss of civilian life
(1,201, of whom 128 were American citizens). There
were strong American protests, and since the German
navy did not have adequate numbers of submarines,
Berlin backed down, and agreed that 'cruiser rules'
would be respected. But in 1916, 108 submarines were
built, together with a new pen for lighter ones at Zeebrugge in Belgium, from where the Channel transports
could be threatened. The navy reckoned at the end of
1916 that it was ready for a new campaign of unrestricted submarine warfare. It presented memoranda, complete with figures, and two of the best-known economists
at Berlin University, Max Sering and Gustav Schmoller,
were brought in to opine as to the damage that would
be done to the British economy. It would collapse, especially if Zeppelins dropped bombs on the grain depots in
the Channel ports, they helpfully added.

Admiral Holtzendorff said that he could sink 600,000 tons of shipping every month, that British shipping would be cut by half, that there would be food riots, and terrible distress in the trading areas. The Chancellor, Bethmann Hollweg, had to take a wider and more sceptical view. He knew in the first place that if Germany declared unrestricted submarine warfare, the United States would almost certainly come into the war. His advisor, Helfferich, could read figures and said that the navy's were a concoction. The new Austrian emperor, Karl, desperate for peace, objected, and the political parties of Left and Centre were also not enthusiastic. But against the military, and with a population that blamed its rat sausages and endless turnips on the British blockade, Bethmann Hollweg could make no headway. Smoking cigarette after cigarette, he tried a manoeuvre to escape from the problem. The four Central Powers declared on 12 December that they would engage upon negotiations over peace. President Wilson's good offices were sought, and he did in fact allow the Germans what appeared to be a safe route for communications to their embassy in Washington. He then enquired as to what the peace terms were to be.

The Allies had no great difficulty: they said that Belgium would have to be restored, that people should have the right to self-determination. Much of this was humbug, and among themselves they were talking about vast extensions of empires, quite without reference to 'self-determination'. The Germans were silent as to their own terms, even when Wilson asked them privately what they had in mind. Bethmann Hollweg could not say that he would restore Belgium, because he did not intend to do so: Germany was fighting for a German Europe, in effect the *Mitteleuropa* programme partly realized at Brest-Litovsk a year later, and Belgium, with its French establishment and British leanings, did not belong. German industrialists were expecting to take over the considerable coal and iron reserves of Belgium, and the military at the very least wanted to take the fortifications of Liège with a view to any future war. The German *Generalgouvernement* in Brussels was also giving guarded encouragement to Flemish separatists, allowing Ghent University to use Flemish, which was regarded in educated circles as peasant stuff – a sort of corrupted Dutch. Bethmann Hollweg was stuck. If he said that Germany was fighting for goodness, beauty and truth, as the Allies claimed that they were doing, he would have been thrown out by a Ludendorff who was now the real master of Germany: the military and the industrialists were working themselves into a fever of annexationism, Belgian coalfields and French iron-ore mines one minute, strips of Poland, to be ethnically cleansed, the next. This left Bethmann Hollweg no alternatives, as regards statements of war aims, beyond silence and lies. British and French diplomats might equally have been embarrassed, and vast imperial plans were being cooked up in secret. But they always had the ostensibly unbeatable argument concerning the restoration of Belgium: at no point did Berlin say it would just restore the country. German diplomats were too clumsy to deal with this situation, and their peace initiative got nowhere. Bethmann Hollweg had no more arguments against the admirals.

On 1 February 1917 a zone around western France and the British Isles was declared open to sinking upon sight. Admiral Holtzendorff, it appeared, was at once proved right. He now had 105 submarines (in June, 129). In January, under 'cruiser rules', 368,000 tons had gone down, 154,000 of them British. In February, 540,000. In March, nearly 600,000 (418,000 British). In April, 881,000 (545,000). The sinkings generally occurred as ships bunched together to reach the ports, at the end of their voyage. Neutrals began to withdraw, ships to be laid up, and American citizens were drowned. To begin with, the British appeared to be helpless; there seemed to be no defence against the submarines. However, Holtzendorff's calculations proved to be wrong – not only wrong, but so far wide of the mark as to make the greatest contribution to Germany's defeat. The British survived; the Americans came in.

Defences were found against U-Boats. The great (New Zealand) physicist Sir Ernest Rutherford was held upside-down from a rowing boat above the Firth of Forth to see if he could hear anything, and eventually a hydrophone was invented, able to detect underwater noise. Depth-charges followed. Destroyers equipped with these things could riposte to submarines, though it meant extraordinary tension on both sides. Brave spirits also suggested to the Admiralty that if ships were placed in a convoy (of twenty ships) then they could be guarded by destroyers. There was absurd resistance – part of the naval establishment clearly not wishing to be held responsible for the doings of merchant captains far beneath them in station. The 'black fortnight' of April, with hundreds of ships down, changed this, and convoy became the rule. After this, sinkings declined, more or less to the number that obtained under 'cruiser rules'. On 10 May, the first convoy sailed, the merchantmen obeyed orders, and the destroyers shepherded them safely across the Atlantic. Only 63 merchantmen were lost of the 5,090 convoyed, and the U-Boats, spending two thirds of their time on voyages to and from port, were hardly more effective than they had been before. But they had conjured up Germany's worst nightmare. The United States entered the war, which meant, in the first instance, that British war finance was saved, and in the second, that blockade worked.

Even after the U-Boat campaign had started, American intervention might not have happened: public opinion was not in favour. It had to be forced. There followed an episode that belongs with the Weber inaugural, the Schlieffen Plan and the Tirpitz fleet in the annals of German self-destructiveness. American intervention – a very large navy, though no army – would have to be countered somehow, thought Berlin. There had, Berlin was aware, been problems with Mexico. Perhaps the Mexicans could be encouraged to attack the United States, upon which Germany would recognize their right to reverse the verdict of the Alamo. Was not Arizona a sort of Mexican Alsace-Lorraine? A telegram was composed, indicating that the Mexicans might be interested in a German alliance; and while they were about it, might they enquire of the Mikado in Japan as to whether he might join the club.

Arthur Zimmermann – the new foreign secretary – sent a telegram to this effect and for good measure sent it along the private line that President Wilson, as a sign of good will, had allowed the Germans to use. British naval intelligence had in fact tapped this American line, and could read German codes (having captured a codebook from an exceedingly brave German expedition through Iran). Great ingenuity was then shown by the British Admiral Hall, who copied the telegram and sent it along a German line that the British knew, and could 'officially' tap. The American ambassador in London was shown the telegram at the end of March. By then, the Americans had broken off diplomatic relations with Berlin (though not with the other Central Powers, and they never did break with Bulgaria). The Zimmermann Telegram reached Congress, and on 6 April, with storms of outraged patriotism, Wilson declared war on Germany. Arthur Zimmermann's telegram was Germany's suicide note, written in farce.

American intervention saved the Allies. The navy helped greatly when it came to extending blockade, but in particular money had become very important indeed. British credit, by the end of 1916, had nearly been exhausted, and the value of sterling really depended upon the willingness of Americans to honour it, at a rate close to five dollars to the pound. The British had been subsidizing Russia – a debt, in the end, of 800 million gold pounds, which for present-day values must be multiplied by forty (it was settled in 1985). Their credit could only be extended if the US government guaranteed it. Now, it did. Raw materials flowed to the Allies. Creating an American army and shipping it to France was another matter, and took months and months. By 1918, 200,000 Americans were arriving every month, but in 1917 men had to be trained, by trainers who themselves knew nothing but boots and saddles. In that sense, Admiral Holtzendorff had been right – the American intervention would not formally matter too much. Nothing would change, provided that the Central Powers could win in 1917.

The British and French did their best to make this possible. General Robert Nivelle almost wrecked the French army, and Field Marshal Sir Douglas Haig did a great deal to wreck the British one as well – the best Scottish general, it was said, in that he killed the most Englishmen. Nivelle was not a fool. This was a war that could be made mobile again if artillery was properly used. There were now thousands of guns and millions of shells, and there were new weapons. Aircraft, in 1914 too liable to break down, and only useful for spotting large bodies of men if the weather was right, were coming into their own. The pilot could now fire at the enemy along the nose of the plane without hitting his own propellors, and single-wing craft were being brought in to replace the slow old biplanes. Aerial photography was now far more accurate, and tanks had been invented. Besides, the gunners' communications improved (on the German side, telephone wire was buried six feet underground) and the 'creeping barrage' was becoming standard: Nivelle reckoned that it would win the war. A barrage that ran just sixty yards ahead of the infantry could silence the enemy until the attackers were within grenade-throwing range, and grenades had also improved. Infantry tactics needed to be changed: no advance in waves, let alone in the great clumps of 1914, but small parties, darting from shell-hole to shell-hole, diagonally, one part firing at the enemy to give cover for the other darting forward.

Nivelle appreciated all of this, and from his Verdun successes thought that he had discovered a formula. He referred to *chablons* ('pulleys'), meaning well-managed mutual support by all arms. Politically and personally he was also suitable. He was Protestant, and Protestants (usually engineers and doctors) were the backbone of the Third Republic, supplying the morality, the education, the spirit – including the Eiffel Tower. His mother was English, and he could charm London lunches (at which – as was ominously said – ladies were present) and explain his methods. Word got back to the Germans that something was impending. Needing to make more economical use of their forces, they shortened the line. The existing western front reflected the events of 1914, and had no logic to it.

It was there because it was there: the front lines back

in 1914 had frozen, as the two sides dug trenches, and all sides held positions that were vulnerable and expensive, purely and simply for reasons of prestige. British Ypres and French Verdun were surrounded on three sides, and the defenders suffered from enfilading fire, but the entire German position was unnecessarily long – troops were needed just to man it who could have been used for better purposes if the line was shortened. It ran, to no strategic value, in a great bulge from the Somme battlefield to the Chemin des Dames on a ridge north-east of Paris. Attacks from there, and from Arras to the north-west, in the British sector, could squeeze the sides of this useless salient. The sensible thing was to shorten the line and use the troops for something more positive. From 9 February to 18 March the Germans withdrew – operation 'Alberich', named after Wagner's nasty dwarf, because cottages were booby-trapped, wells were poisoned and trees were 'ringed'. The Allies moved into shattered territory, with no opportunity for its reconstitution. The withdrawal also wrecked Nivelle's original plans, which had been based on careful calculation of German gun positions. Now, he had to do the homework all over again, and he had placed his reputation on the line: he was a newcomer, with a reputation to keep up, and to give up there and then would have been a shattering blow. The nightmare had to follow its course. In an effort to keep front-line morale high, he had decided to inform the troops directly of his plans. A copy of them was found on a sergeant whom the Germans captured in a trench raid.

The British were supposed to drain off German reserves in the first instance, by an attack at Arras, and there was a considerable success on 9 April, when the Canadians captured Vimy ridge, the British emerging from concealment in the old cellars of the Burgundian town, and surprising a German defence that had ineptly allowed much of its strength to be shattered by careful bombardment of the front positions. Then Haig, as was his wont, battered on on foot as the Germans arrived by train, and failed to make any progress – even, for six weeks, keeping cavalry hanging around, clogging the roads, in the hope of some glad morning. Arras was a sign that a new type of warfare was emerging, in that the gunners now disposed of formidable quantities of shell, and knew how to use it. However, there were considerable problems with rear organization, and Nivelle's relations with Haig became poor, the former intimating in contemptuous language that the British army was demanding too much of the railway network and squandering resources. In this, he was probably right, but picking a quarrel was not a sensible thing to do at that moment. Lloyd George, who mistrusted Haig, exploited the affair to put him under Nivelle's orders, and was himself discredited when Nivelle's own doings proved calamitous.

This they duly did. The attack on 16 April against the Chemin des Dames meant driving Senegalese troops into a sleety blizzard, with a bombardment that the Germans had foreseen enough to keep their troops away from the dangerous zones. Nivelle had promised,

as part of the formula, that he would break off the attack
if he did not succeed in the first two days. He failed
everywhere, except east of Rheims, and persisted with
the attack, with predictable effect. By now, well-
connected junior officers were able to tell deputies of the
National Assembly how things were at the front, and
the politicians had anyway only really accepted Nivelle
because they thought he could play the British. And then
came one of twentieth-century France's encounters with
reality: the troops rebelled – refusing to go any more
into the charnel houses that their generals were expecting
them to confront. Later on, when Communists were
using certain episodes of the First World War as propaganda, the French mutinies of 1917 (like the Italian
collapse somewhat later) became evidence that the
working classes and the peasantry were rebelling. The
matter was not so simple: a careful French historian,
Guy Pedroncini,[1] reckoned that about 40,000 of the men
had been involved, those closest to the front, and had
resumed discipline when talked to by sensible officers.
Nivelle himself was soon dismissed, and the new commander, Philippe Pétain, had some sense of how morale
might be restored: only forty-nine men were executed,
and matters regarding leave and supply were made more
humane. Did they want a German occupation? No. If
they deserted, their womenfolk told them to go back.
The army came back to order, but its generals had
learned. Pétain appreciated that he must stick to small,
competently organized operations, and these were
indeed well staged. For instance the 'Laffaux salient',

part of the Chemin des Dames, was taken back in October. For France, it would be *jusqu'au bout*, and an old radical nationalist, Clemenceau, took office.

But in that same Nivelle spring, there began another mutiny, this time on an enormous scale: the Russian army was breaking up. The German calculation of 1914, that Russia could be defeated then, but not in a few years, was, in its own terms, perfectly accurate. By 1916 her output of war goods was at least adequate. What was not adequate was the organization that more advanced countries could show as regards transport, rationing, finance, national unity. The great cities filled up with refugees, and peasants crowded the trains as they migrated to find work; at the same time, the army's demands on transport were such that trains were fewer, and the capital got only fifty grain wagons a day of the ninety it had had before the war. Privation, universally shared, might be tolerable. But some had fuel and food, and others did not; there was suspicion that Germans were everywhere in the woodwork, including the Tsar's glowering spouse; and the 'capitalists' who coined it in from war work in Petrograd – as the capital had been, anti-Germanly, re-named – generally had foreign names. How do such situations turn fatal? Again, the inevitable accident. 8 March (23 February by the then Russian, religious, calendar) was International Women's Day, and the working-class wives of the capital staged a demonstration against the rising price of bread. They were having to get up early, in freezing cold, and wait around, only to discover often enough that the bakery did not have fuel for the flour, or that the flour was being held back by 'speculators' in expectation of a price rise. In the first week of March the weather, which had been very cold, suddenly improved, which allowed demonstrations to go ahead.

Again true to form for the Russia of that era, the Tsarist machinery for repression was altogether inadequate: not even glue for posters proclaiming martial law. As George Orwell remarked of eighteenth-century England, there was nothing between putting up your shutters and calling out the army. Briefly, the police attempted to control things, and a few martyrs resulted. Then the army was called out. But it now consisted of unwilling conscripts, living in giant barracks in the middle of the government quarter, and they were disaffected, smuggling in drink, getting close to the working-class women. In a more advanced country, such soldiers would have been housed on some Salisbury Plain, but old Russia could not have afforded the infrastructure. The troops, invited to fire at the crowds, struck on 27 February (12 March). Authority now collapsed. The streets were full of soldiers, charging around in lorries, waving red flags.

Next day, the uniquely Russian feature of the revolution appeared: a *soviet*, the Russian word for 'council'. On 28 February, the factories and the soldiers elected representatives for a sort of glorified strike committee, soon dominated by socialist intellectuals, with an addiction to the sound of their own voices. There were also politicians in the Russian parliament, the Duma, who thought that they must take charge, and by now many of the generals were on their side. One thing was essential: to get rid of Tsar Nicholas II, whom everyone, including the Imperial Yacht Club on one of the grandest streets of Petrograd, *Morskaya*, regarded as a liability. The generals told him to go, which he did on 2 (15) March, and the Duma politicians set up a 'provisional government', eventually proclaiming Russia a democratic republic, though they shrank from a proper election. The Soviet was the representative body, and had the key, but did not know what to do with it: 3,000 people, crowding into the Tauride Palace, two thirds of them soldiers. An executive committee was set up, composed of socialist intellectuals, incapable of organizing. It was, again, a feature of Russia's peculiar state of development, at the time, that the stiffening which other, later, popular revolutions immediately acquired – from the trade unions – was mainly absent. Trade unions might have their quarrels with the bosses, but did not want order to break down, and had the muscle to exert themselves, even in conditions nearing anarchy. Outside printers and railwaymen, there were no Russian trade unions. Meanwhile the socialist intelligentsia made sure that 'reaction' would be made harmless: they arranged for an end to saluting, to the military death penalty, and decreed that anyone and everyone in the army should form committees to elect officers and supervise their doings.

But the causes of the revolution did not go away – on

the contrary, matters worsened. One of the great engines present in any real revolution (there have been some surreal ones) was inflation. Russian public finance now collapsed. In 1914 a very strict policy had been followed, and even the Tsar licked his own stamps, to save money. But the war became extraordinarily expensive, and the government was at a loss. It damaged its own cause early on, decreeing that spirits would not be drunk: one third of its revenue had come from the vodka monopoly. There was not the machinery for an income tax, nor was there a large middle class from which to take War Loan, as elsewhere. The government therefore issued paper money at a greater and greater rate – so great, in the end, that the printing presses broke down and, when clients came to banks to cash cheques, they were handed bundles of large notes with instructions to ink in the numbers themselves. The zeros on the notes went up, and so did the zeros on the price-tags. Food stocks became unpredictable: they might be held back at every stage in the chain, from peasant producers getting useless paper to banks which hoarded sugar in their vaults because at least it was a store of value. In turn, this problem affected transport, as railway wagons went to parts of the country that traditionally supplied grain and returned half-empty, while in other parts of the country food rotted for want of transport. In the summer of 1917, there was a spiralling down of problems that meshed in an indissoluble web. Nothing worked. Government and Soviet struck attitudes, talked. Into this situation, on 9 (22) April, stepped Lenin, the most extreme figure in Russian affairs. He and his followers – called 'Bolsheviks' because, years before, in order to take over the Social Democrat newspaper in exile, he had under-handedly created a majority at the meeting in question, the Russian word for 'majority' being *bolshinstvo* – could see a simple solution, where other men saw none at all. Lenin said: bread for the people, land to the peasant, peace to all peoples. If the Russians started the process by getting out of this war, then others would follow – especially the Germans, among whom Lenin had lived for many a year. Then everything else could be sorted out. This suited the German government, and it let him travel from Switzerland to Russia by train.[2]

Lenin had an extraordinarily powerful character. His charisma does not show up in his writings, which are unreadable, and, even granted the difference in rhetoric between one civilization and another, it is difficult to see how Russians could be held captive by his oratory. But they seem to have been, and, certainly, in a small group, Lenin prevailed against considerable initial hostility: in April 1917, even Bolsheviks returning from prison camps were in favour of carrying on with the war. Lenin spoke, and events went his way. The old order, as he said, would make mistakes, and indeed it did – its finances a mess, the food queues out of control, the generals feeling hopelessly inferior to the Germans, the troops sitting doing nothing but drink evil stuff on empty stomachs, the bankers and the diplomats in thrall to Anglo-French imperialists. The Russian Revolution was a huge mutiny, and though the army did stay at the front, in the summer of 1917 it was quite incapable of offensive action and only barely capable of defensive. Briefly, in August, the Provisional Government tried to put down the Bolsheviks, but even then there was muddle. Lenin sat it out in Finland, in thin disguise. When a 'state conference' was held in the Bolshoy Theatre in Moscow, to discuss Russia's future, even the buffets were on strike. As the autumn went ahead, the only organized body left was the Soviet, by now Bolshevik-dominated, and on 7 November its troops put an end to the Government. More people died in the crush of the tenth-anniversary film than in the actual 'seizure of power'.

How were the Allies to react to the mounting trouble in Russia? The Americans were far from ready, and the French were licking their wounds. The Italians, in August, launched the eleventh battle of the Isonzo, advanced five miles over the Bainsizza plateau north of Trieste, suffered twice as many casualties as the Austrians, and stopped. Only the British had the strength for a great effort, and in the summer, in Flanders, they went ahead. It was partly to do with Russia, and also partly to do with the Americans, in that the general aim was to win the war and impose a British peace before President Wilson could muddy the waters. Lloyd George subsequently distanced himself from the venture, but in fact allowed it to happen. It has entered history as 'Passchendaele', the name of a small village on a ridge that had some local tactical significance. After three months, and 400,000 casualties, the British took it. It was arguably the lowest point of British strategy.

Haig had always really wanted to advance in Flanders, and this in itself made sense. The Ypres salient was not easily defensible, and there were 7,000 casualties each week because of 'normal wastage' – the Germans occupied a height, the Messines ridge, and could fire at Ypres from the side. But from Ypres to the Dutch border – the capture, in other words, of the Belgian coast – was not far, and the submarine base at Zeebrugge could be dealt with. The plan itself was not senseless, and the British by now had considerable experience with the kind of bombardment that might loosen the defence. They also had the strength – millions of shells. But the whole area was known as the Low Countries for a very good reason: it had been rescued from the sea, the water-table was close to the surface, and if it were churned up by shell, there would be mud. If there were rain, it would be a morass.

Still, as so often, generals were lured into disaster by an initial success. In an epic of doggedness, miners had tunnelled below the Messines ridge, and had twenty-one great mines to blow up under it, with a million tons of explosives. Infantry had been carefully trained, with scale models of the ridge, and the local army commander, Plumer of the Second, was a careful, prudent man who paid attention to detail and was without grandiose ambitions. On 7 June the mines were blown – an explosion heard in London – and a vast bombardment silenced the German batteries. The Germans collapsed and withdrew, which gave the British high ground from which to fire, and it made their supply-lines to Ypres more secure. As ever, though, after such initial successes, the attack petered out. Haig threw away the advantage.

There was then an extraordinary interval before the next British attack – an interval lasting until 31 July, during which the German defences were strengthened, in the formidable, sophisticated way that was then becoming second nature – five or six miles of intensive digging, with concrete 'pill-boxes' (the British name for them) in which heavy machine-guns were placed, in such a way as to stitch a web of fire-lines that would be deadly (and unexpected) for attackers. These defences required some cunning. If the front line were too thinly held, the defenders might become demoralized, supposing that they were meant to be sacrificed. If they were too thickly held, the defenders would be wiped out by the concentrated fire that generally ended a sophisticated bombardment (the Russians calculated that it took 25,000 rounds to cut a small hole in wire obstacles). The seven-week pause between Messines and the opening of 'Third Ypres', as the British offensive was called, meant that the German defence expert, a Colonel von Lossberg, could do his best, with six separate defensive positions. The front position consisted of three lines, breast-works with parapets rather than elaborate trenches. They were 200 yards apart, manned by a few infantry companies. Two thousand yards back was the second position, with concrete pill-boxes to shelter the support battalions, and between the first and second positions there were more pill-boxes, with heavy machine-guns. This was 'the forward battle zone'. A mile back was another system, sheltering reserve battalions. Then a third position, another mile back, where the decisive events were expected to occur, the 'greater battle zone'.

'Third Ypres' was to do more to disaffect the British educated classes than anything that Lenin ever wrote. Haig was unlucky, in the sense that it rained more than usual, though students of the weather could have told him that rain did happen in those parts. The initial bombardment, starting in the middle of July, went on for two weeks, and of course gave the Germans notice of what was to come: no surprise. Nine attacking divisions faced five, but the weather had been so bad that aerial reconnaissance was impossible, and 'sound ranging', an ingenious method of detecting the whereabouts of an enemy battery from the sound-wave of its firing, did not work. The bombardment, 'of unprecedented ferocity', was not very accurate: 4,300,000 shells were fired, but German guns placed behind the Passchendaele ridge were unharmed, and sixty-four strongpoints remained intact to confront the attackers' left and centre. When the attack started, at 3.50 a.m. on 31 July, low and stormy cloud obscured the rising sun, and since the bombardment had destroyed the front positions, the infantry got forward in some areas, but not on the central and right areas where a continuation of the Messines ridge, the Gheluvelt plateau, had to be taken if German artillery were not to enjoy a continuous advantage of height. The creeping barrage was in places lost, and signalling, given the weather, did not make clear where the front line even was. Even so, the first day was not unsuccessful – no first day of the Somme. Had the objective simply been to take the ridges around the Ypres salient that made life so difficult there, the operation might have made some sense. But Haig was ambitious for a breakthrough, and clogged up the supply-lines, as ever, with useless cavalry; and Gough, of the Fifth Army, believed in 'hurroush', the gallant advance. This translated, in practice, into a plod through the mire.

There followed one of the most extraordinary episodes of this or any other war. Rain fell on the first day, and carried on for seven days. In August, there were only three rainless days. It fell and fell, twice the average for the month. Heavy shelling made the problem far worse, because the battlefield and the routes towards it turned into quagmires. If wounded men fell off the cart taking them to the rear, they drowned. A field-ambulance sergeant wrote: 'it requires six men to every stretcher, two of these being constantly employed helping the others out of the holes; the mud is in some cases up to our waists. A couple of journeys . . . and the strongest men are ready to collapse.' When even the lightest field artillery had to be moved to escape from German fire, the mud was so thick that moving a single gun just 250 yards took six and a half hours. Wounded men who had crawled into shell-holes for safety found that the rain caused the water in them to rise and rise, so that they could see their own deaths by drowning approaching, fractions of an inch at a time. In this, Gough launched his August attacks, failing miserably again and again.

Plumer was then given his hand. He insisted on a degree of reinforcement that had been refused to Gough, and proposed only very limited operations – the 'bite and hold' principle. Troops should just take their initial objective and have their positions strengthened, rather than attempt to advance any further, beyond the artillery's capacity and preparation. Plumer was also lucky, in a way that Gough never was: the weather cleared, and the ground began to harden again, though never sufficiently. Three limited battles followed in early autumn – that for the village of Broodseinde being the best known – and they were marked by creeping barrages of great intensity, keeping a curtain of shells just ahead of the attackers, reaching only up to 1,000 yards ahead, with the infantry keeping careful step. German counter-attacks were broken up by such a bombardment, and the troops, not too far from their own positions, could count on reasonable backup. The Germans had no answer to such tactics, and Plumer's limited operations (like Pétain's in the same period) were a success. But they did only cover 3,000 yards, with immense effort, and at that rate the war would never be won. Still, Haig started dreaming again, and was somehow convinced that German morale was cracking, that the Germans would soon be surrendering in droves. He ordered Plumer to continue; and then the rain started again. Throughout October and in the first half of November, the troops concentrated on the insignificant village of Passchendaele, and finally clawed their way through the mud to take it – an advance that created a thin salient which everyone knew would have to be evacuated if ever there was a serious counter-attack. A senior staff officer at last visited the battlefield, towards the very end. As he approached, he burst into tears, and asked the driver, 'Did we send the men into *that*?' When warned by his own intelligence chief that the Germans were not cracking, Haig added a characteristic note: the man was a Catholic and therefore was perhaps getting information from tainted sources. However, Haig did at least have a faith in ultimate victory, and did not lose heart. The year ended with events that pre-figured the end of the war – Cambrai.

Here at last the tank experts were allowed their heads. They had said that tanks would be effective if employed together in large numbers, and on hard ground, with proper artillery support. Air support was beginning to matter, as well, because it could force the defenders to keep their heads down, or even just to look elsewhere – the beginnings of the *Blitzkrieg* techniques that were to win battles in 1918. There were also techniques open to gunners that had not been available before. The most important target of guns was the enemy guns. Earlier, these had to be identified from the air or by their own shots, and artillery used against them would have to be registered, that is, ranging shots fired, which both stopped surprise and identified the hostile gun-position. Now, after aerial reconnaissance (itself much more professional, with proper photography) the enemy gun could be marked on a grid map, and the artillery assault on it therefore prepared in theory without practice shots.

In other words, at Cambrai the British gained surprise. The attack went in on 20 November and won an immediate success, with a considerable advance and a large capture of prisoners and guns. In England, the church bells were rung. The advance went far ahead, as usual beyond its supply-lines, and even into open country at last. But the German commander was an able man, who organized a counter-attack on the new principles used in the East – specially trained 'storm troops', moving fast, using grenades, and avoiding strongpoints. The German counter-attack could have been held had the British had reserves, but there were none – Passchendaele had seen to that.

At the same moment in late October, again using the new principles, came what was the most brilliant victory of the entire war, with the possible exception of Brusilov's – brilliant in the sense that brains and determination overcame material weakness. By summer 1917 astute German gunners had also worked out the principles known to the British, but they applied these principles more thoroughly. Guns could vary in range and direction; or wind and rain might affect the firing. Each one was therefore tested on firing ranges to check for variations, so that due allowance might be made. The bombardment was not designed to smash defences, but mainly to neutralize the command system, the movement of reserves, by a hurricane of shelling and gas. The new methods were tried out at Riga on 1 September, with thirteen divisions assaulting Russian positions on the Dvina, upstream from the city. There was complete surprise; the reserves, generally so fatal for an exhausted attacker, could not come in because a 'box' bombardment isolated the defensive area, with a steady curtain of fire to prevent the reserves from coming up. There were new infantry tactics as well. Each army acquired a specially trained assault battalion, carrying light machine-guns and flamethrowers; its task was to move fast ahead, in a loose skirmishing line. The counter-attack at Cambrai had succeeded through these methods, and at Riga they had also shown their value if combined with the new type of bombardment. Commanders who understood such methods were now transferred from the Russian front to others.

In this case, Italy. Not unlike Russia, she had much that was ancient and much that was modern, but a great part of her people were still in a localized, peasant world – one third of the soldiers were illiterate. Her rulers had pushed the country into war, making her run in the hope that she would learn to walk. They had expected an easy trot to Vienna, and had hardly advanced beyond the customs-posts; subsequent offensives had brought twice as many casualties to the Italians as to the Austrians but had only occasionally brought any kind of gain. There were eleven separate battles on the north-eastern border – the river Isonzo (now, in Slovenia, the Soca) – and, as the Italians learned about guns, and the Austrians became tired, there were successes of a fairly modest kind. However, as with Haig's doings, these gains came at an enormous cost – one and a half million casualties, as against 600,000 Austrian. In the eleventh battle, where part of the Bainsizza plateau was taken, the Italians lost 170,000 men, 40,000 of them killed.

For this, the military establishment were inclined to blame the men. Somewhat as in Russia, there was an enormous gap between officer class and men, and the north Italian Cadorna, who ran the strategy (he was the son of the man who bundled the Pope into the Vatican when Italy was united), reckoned that his men would only fight if terrorized. If men did not get out of their trenches to attack, their own guns must fire on them. After the war, monuments to the Unknown Soldier went up in Paris and London – men who had been blown to pieces of bone and could no longer be identified, with widows of such men chosen at random for an opening ceremony. The Italians had such a monument, but the area where the Second Army fought was excluded from the search for unidentified remains, because any soldier there might have been killed by his own generals. One such officer, who became head of the Fascist militia (and was probably murdered in revenge, thrown from a train, in 1931) used to take his stand in the front trenches, with his revolver, shooting down his own men if they hesitated. Cadorna even adopted the Roman practice of decimation, shooting every tenth man at random in a regiment that had done badly. There were some cases of extraordinary cruelty – for instance, a father of seven shot for being the last to go on parade because he had overslept, this in a brigade that had been cut off in no man's land, had tried to surrender, had been rescued, after an otherwise commendable record, and was now supposed to be punished. When, in August 1917, the Pope launched his peace appeal, at a time when the entire intervention of Italy could easily be judged to have been a dreadful blunder, Cadorna banned the Italian press at the front.

He was about to receive retribution. The Bainsizza affair had scared the Germans: what if Austria dropped out? With the end of the war in the east, troops were freed for other purposes, and a new German army was set up, the Fourteenth, under the competent Otto von Below, who knew about the Riga methods. His force contained two future field marshals, Rommel and Schörner, both of whom distinguished themselves, this time as junior officers capturing mountains. Seven German and five good Austrian divisions mustered on the upper Isonzo, in very mountainous territory, after a display of virtuosity with transport of which, in this war, the Germans and French alone were capable (the very delivery of milk to Vienna schools had to be suspended). Over railways of limited capacity, and then over narrow mountain roads, a thousand guns with a thousand rounds each were delivered, and with Porsche's traction machines and four-wheel drives, or ingenious manoeuvring of monstrous instruments of war through mineshafts, the Central Powers established formidable local superiority without the Italians' taking it at all seriously, though deserters warned them.

The record of the interrogation of the deserters was found on the floor of Italian headquarters in Udine a few days later; by then, catastrophe had occurred. Relative success on the Bainsizza plateau, in the middle of the Isonzo front, had pushed part of the Italian army uncomfortably forward; there was an Austrian bridgehead at Tolmein (Tolmino), and the enormous Italian army corps in the area occupied a position divided by the river; its commander – curiously enough the General Badoglio who later had a prominent role first for and then against Italian Fascism – clearly did not know whether to put the weight on the eastern, attacking bank or the western, defending one. In any event, chased by a German bombardment, he ended up in a cave, not able to direct either part. To his north was an army corps centred on an Isonzo village called Flitsch (Plezzo, now Bovec). Entirely unexpected, five of the best Austrian divisions were going to come down a mountain at that corps. Downriver was another little place, Caporetto,[3] marking the join of the two main Italian units. Neither was ready. Cadorna himself had had some notion that he ought probably to go over to the defensive. However, Capello, commander of the main Isonzo army – the Second – had other ideas, and for a month, delayed preparations: if the Central Powers attacked, he would counter-attack, he said, and held his troops forward. Cadorna was scared of Capello – a volcanic little Neapolitan Freemason, of none too grand social origins. He tolerated the disobedience, and when the Central Powers struck, Italian artillery was being hauled into defensive positions at last, wending a wearisome way through the middle of retreating troops.

On 24 October at 2 a.m. the guns opened up. The German expert, a Brigadier von Berendt, understood how to organize the mixture of gas – which killed the mules transporting guns – and high explosive. Since there was air superiority, the Germans knew where the Italian batteries were, and silenced most of them. The bombardment waxed and waned – a pause, around 4.30, for an hour, to gull the enemy into taking some fresh air, then more intensive fire, then, in the last fifteen minutes, 'drum-fire', including the dropping of shell by trench-mortars on the front positions, which were utterly wrecked. At 8 a.m. the attackers moved. On the Flitsch side, the Austrians came down a mountain and the Italian defenders had no gas masks. The Austrians then went ahead through a valley to the plains not far beyond. The general in charge of the Italian corps (he had only four divisions to cover twenty miles of complicated front) ordered a retreat, and also a counter-attack. One of his divisional generals, wondering what was happening, drove into the village of Caporetto to use a working telephone. He was captured, because the other element of the Central Powers' attack had broken through Badoglio's confused positions and swung north-west, along the river, to Caporetto. The division then disintegrated, as did the northern corps altogether.

At Tolmein, there was an extraordinary feat of arms. German mountain troops had to seize some commanding heights, which meant a climb, after the bombardment, of 900 metres. Rommel, then just a captain, with 200 men of the Württemberg Mountain Battalion showed the German army at its best. He did not try a direct attack on the ridge of the Kolovrat, the massive mountain on the western side of the river. Instead, he sent a group of eight men under a corporal to see if there was a way through the defences. There was. Italian sentries were sheltering from the rain, and were captured. There was a gap beyond in the wire. Another dug-out was taken, and Rommel's men crept up to the ridge. Then they moved along it – the Italians so surprised that one battery of heavy guns was captured from behind, while the officers were at lunch and the men were playing cards. Then Rommel moved on the southern side of the ridge, inviting surrender. One after another, he took the better part of five Italian regiments. In spirit, it was the same performance as he was to put up in the summer of 1942, when he wrapped cardboard tank-like structures round Volkswagen cars, drove to the great British base at Tobruk, bombarded it into surrendering, and took such quantities of petrol from it that he was able to drive on, almost to Cairo. In the Caporetto battle, another officer of his regiment also captured a mountain and was awarded the highest possible decoration. Rommel's commanding officer asked for Rommel to be given the medal too, and was told that that decoration could not possibly be given twice to the same unit at the same moment. Rommel captured another mountain and the rule had to be broken.

On 25 October the Italian position had collapsed and the generals started looking for excuses. Capello played the sickness game: full of energy one moment at the best hotel in Verona, stricken at Padua hospital the next. Badoglio hastened to pin the blame on him, and hid. Only the Duke of Aosta, commanding the Third Army to the south, kept his head and retreated in reasonable order. Cadorna himself, on the 27th, composed the most remarkable document sent by any general in this war, claiming that the Second Army had simply not fought at all and that 'the Reds' were infiltrating the country. The government suppressed the telegram, but not before it had been sent abroad. When the British and French were asked for direct help, they made the dismissal of Cadorna a pre-condition, a demand most reluctantly conceded by the Italian establishment; in that army, as in the Russian, duds were adhesive, and were even able to influence official histories (the true story did not emerge until 1967).

Guns were captured wholesale as they were man-oeuvred around narrow passes; soldiers, in droves, surrendered out of utter bewilderment when they found Austrians and Germans coming along paths in the rear, where they had never been expected at all; Cadorna muddled things further, when he mismanaged retreat. There were four bridges over the river Tagliamento, which marked the opening of the great Friulian plain, some twenty miles from the Isonzo front line, along roads flanked by huge mountains. Two of these bridges were assigned to the Third Army, which withdrew over the river in reasonable order. Parts of the Second Army had to struggle north-west, coinciding with refugees, and found one of the bridges captured; over the other there was a disorganized mass evacuation, with, on the other side of the river, pot-bellied little colonels shooting any man apparently straggling. The episode was described in one of the famous books about this part of the war, Ernest Hemingway's *A Farewell to Arms*.[4] In the event, there were 300,000 prisoners and 300,000 *sbandati* – men who had lost their units – and half of the entire artillery of the Italian army was captured. An attempt was made to stand on the Tagliamento, but the attackers' artillery, thanks to Porsche, was being manoeuvred quite fast; the retreat went on to the river Piave and, on the western side, the *massif* of Monte Grappa. British and French troops arrived. So did malaria, from the marshes of the area. The front was now much shorter – seventy miles, as against 180 – and the Central Powers' forces were by now a very long way from railheads, themselves inadequate. In Italy, national resistance at last became popular. The sensible Diaz succeeded Cadorna, and the Italian High Command stopped treating their soldiery as cattle; the Austrians and Germans could not break the Piave and Grappa positions. On 2 December the Caporetto offensive was officially halted, and Otto von Below was sent to the western front, where the offensive of all offensives was about to begin. The German leadership had not quite managed to knock out Italy. But they were now given an enormous advantage: Russia collapsed.

NOTES

1. Guy Pedroncini, *Les mutineries de 1917* (Paris, 1967).
2. Lenin had an extraordinary intermediary, Helfand, a one-time revolutionary (code-named 'Parvus') who had made a fortune out of the Young Turks and taken over the Ottoman tobacco monopoly (he lived in the house, on an island in the Sea of Marmara, where Lenin's principal lieutenant, Trotsky, was exiled by Stalin in 1929). He fixed the Germans, who wanted chaos in Russia and arranged for Lenin and his followers to travel through Germany to Stockholm (where the go-between was Kurt Riezler) by the first no-smoking train in history, Lenin being fanatical about this as well. Then it was arrival at the Finland Station in Petrograd, on 16 April, after a week's travel, with a ceremonial welcome.
3. It gave its name to the battle, not altogether accurately. There is an excellent Slovene museum in the town, now called Kobarid (German name, Karfreit).
4. Hemingway did not in fact reach Italy until 1918.

WWI

preceding pages: British Mark IV tank

On the very day the Caporetto offensive was officially halted, a Bolshevik delegation arrived to arrange an armistice at Brest-Litovsk, the headquarters of the German army in the east, a town ruined in the retreat of 1915, few of its major buildings usable. To begin with, the Bolsheviks had supposed that, if they just appealed for peace, the ordinary soldiers would throw down their arms and call it a day. Trotsky announced that his foreign policy would be 'to launch a few proclamations and then shut up shop'. He published the 'secret treaties' – the agreements, which he found in the archives, as to the carving up of the world by the Entente. However, despite some fraternization and, somewhat later, some sympathetic strikes, 'imperialism', as the Bolsheviks saw it, did not collapse. The Russian army had disintegrated, the capital was in chaos, and the soldiers were going home, 'voting with their feet', as Lenin said. There was not much else that the Bolsheviks could do but negotiate an armistice and hope that the propaganda would strike a chord in the war-weary of all nations. Their rather motley gathering, peasant and all, arrived at Brest-Litovsk, there to be treated to another of those surreal scenes that marked the German war effort: a banquet, the peasant sitting between Austrian aristocrats who asked him about the planting of onions. The armistice was arranged, and terms of peace were discussed.

These discussions were interminable, at times philosophical, at times historical: both sides were playing for time, the Germans in the expectation that the non-Russian peoples of the Tsarist empire would declare independence, the Bolsheviks in the expectation of universal revolution. In the event, the Germans delivered an ultimatum, signed a separate peace treaty with the Ukraine, marched in to protect their new satellite, and moved forward into territory vacated by Russian soldiers, especially in the Baltic regions. For the Central Powers, expecting that the blockade would be tightened, the resources of these areas mattered greatly, and for the Austrians – the population of Vienna below the bread line – it was a matter of life and death. Would the Bolsheviks recognize the satellite states – Finland, Georgia, the Ukraine, and so on? Lenin persuaded the Bolsheviks: go back to the Russian heartland, recoup, and wait to see what happens. He persuaded them, and on 3 March the Bolsheviks signed a treaty that turned much of Tsarist Russia into a huge German protectorate. General von Eichhorn ran the Ukraine; General von Lossow wandered into Georgia, to control the oil of the Trans-Caucasus; there were plans for U-Boats to be transported to the Caspian itself. Ludendorff talked of invading British India; Otto-Günther von Wesendonck, grandson of the woman who had inspired Wagner's songs of that name, opined that 'even the idea of a German land-route to China can no longer be dismissed as fantasy.'[1] Would this last? It depended upon the western front.

Forty divisions were now transferred from east to west. This gave Germany superiority at least until the Americans arrived – a process that took the Allies time, and even disrupted the trade in vital raw materials. The war-economic position of Germany was now such that her alternatives were outright victory or outright collapse. The Hindenburg programme had involved an enormous effort, with huge investments in machinery and factories. Output was at its maximum. But it was at the expense of the longer term: the railway network was starting to give out, so was agricultural machinery and industrial plant. If the war were not speedily ended, Germany would plunge. There was a clear choice: to make the last great effort at outright victory, or try for peace. In fact, around this time came the only really serious move towards a general agreement, when Kühlmann, the foreign secretary, hinted to the British that Germany might give up Belgium in return for a free hand in the east. Niall Ferguson rightly says that at this moment the Allies' morale was lower than at any other point in the war. It has also rightly been remarked that, since about 1850, there has only really been one question in British foreign policy: Germany or Russia? A few despairing conservatives and some farsighted socialists might agree, in the end, on Germany. They were isolated: every measure of public opinion shows huge support for war to the bitter end, and Lloyd George, after some hesitation, responded to it. He would be The Man Who Won the War, not The Man Who Made the Peace. He said himself: a Germany running Russia would be unbeatable; would swallow up everything else. And in any case, there was America; and by now other states were queuing up to declare war on Germany, with a view to taking over ships and property. Lloyd George told his allies about Kühlmann's approach, and declared that he regarded the French claim to Alsace-Lorraine as a British war aim. Kühlmann became enraged. It did him no good: Ludendorff soon engineered his dismissal, and he was replaced by Admiral von Hintze, who did what he was told. The might-have-been peace ran into the sand; there would be no British representative at Brest-Litovsk. Much ink has been spent on peace initiatives during the war, but Kühlmann's was the only serious one from Berlin. President Wilson also produced a plan that was serious: the 'Fourteen Points', in essence about the self-determination of nations. The Germans at Brest-Litovsk could have accepted these then adapted them in detail. Instead they went ahead for outright victory.

On the ground, it looked very promising. Recent battles – Riga, Cambrai, Caporetto – had shown that the German army had found a method of restoring mobility to the battlefield, and the professional talent of generals such as von Below, von der Marwitz and von Hutier, the architects of these victories, was beyond compare. Besides, the Germans in the west now had superiority of numbers. There had been 147 German divisions in the west as against 178 Allied ones. There were now 191 German divisions, thanks to the Russian collapse: 137,000 officers, three and a half million men, with the horses to keep matters mobile, at least at the start. In other words, the German superiority could be concentrated, with crushing effect, at any single spot on the line (as had been achieved at Caporetto). A set of operations, with code-names, was planned, and the first, named after the Archangel, was 'Michael'. Other code-names, for parts of the German line, came from Wagner's *Ring* – 'Siegfried', 'Kriemhild', 'Hunding-Brünnhild', for example.

Common sense dictated that, if you were attacking two enemies, you attacked the join, where their armies met. Each enemy would look after himself, maybe retreating in different directions – in this case, the French to cover Paris and the British the Channel ports, from which they could get away to England. This had nearly happened back in 1914. Now, the British joined up with the French just beyond the old Somme battlefields, around St Quentin. Between there and Arras, to the north, stood the British Fifth Army, commanded by Gough, a gallant man with a history of bad luck. Only nine of some fifty British divisions had not undergone the miseries of Passchendaele, and morale was not brilliant. Officers noticed that the men no longer sang the (superb) songs that they had made up earlier. The mood in the

British army was a characteristic, 'we're here because we're here because we're here because we're here'.

Besides, the new principles of this war were not so well understood on the British side as on the German. Otto von Below, especially, understood how to combine infantry and artillery, as at Caporetto. He was now moved to northern France, for Ludendorff's offensive. But if offensive techniques had now been vastly improved, so, too, had defensive ones. The new principle was 'defence in depth'; Passchendaele had been a model of it. Gough and his staff had not absorbed the logic of it, for various reasons – partly because they did not have the numbers of men required, partly because they still reckoned that a strong front line was in itself a good thing, partly because they did not trust their men to make complicated manoeuvres under fire, partly because they underestimated the Germans (who were supposed to have been demoralized by Passchendaele), but mainly because of a very British notion that things would be all right on the night. Nearly 90 per cent of Gough's battalions were within 3,000 yards of the front line, far too close to enemy artillery. But there was a deeper weakness. The British had suffered 800,000 casualties in 1917, and were again under a million in strength; after Passchendaele, the men were not inclined to trust the staff, and the general reserve, of eight divisions, was in the north, in Flanders. The Americans had begun to arrive, but they had not been trained and had only a single division ready for battle. Finally, Haig himself, surrounded by creepy young officers, helping him on and off with his coat – like Cadorna before Caporetto – showed no signs at all of worry. Why should the Germans, if they did attack, do any better than he himself had done?

Ludendorff performed prodigies of concentration, by stealth. He brought up 750,000 men – seventy-six divisions against twenty-six (300,000). He also brought up three quarters of the entire artillery of the western front – 6,600 guns – giving a superiority of three to one. The new weaponry was to hand – light machine-guns, portable by one or two soldiers, grenades that could be fired from a rifle rather than thrown by hand – and infantry tactics could therefore become much more flexible. The German army's greatest strength lay in the profusion of non-commissioned officers – sergeants and corporals (Hitler was one, and he got two Iron Crosses for bravery). These were men who, without being officers, knew how to command small bodies, whereas in other armies you had to have an officer (in the Russian case, even now, they man the telephones). There was a special school in Belgium to train infantry that would move forward, fast, dodging and weaving, giving each other cover fire. Such were the *Stosstrupps*. They were not to try and deal with enemy posts but to move forward and destroy communications. Enemy forces holding out would be covered by other troops, not similarly trained. But there were other advantages for the attackers. Aircraft had come into their own, and the Germans could photograph British gun positions and identify them from a map reference without registering through a gunnery observer. There were now 2,600 aircraft, some metal and single-wing.

The British Fifth Army was to face this extraordinary machinery. It then had a final piece of bad luck – Gough's fate. The guns opened up on 21 March at 4.40 a.m. and it was a very foggy morning. The British gunners could not see what they were doing. The German bombardment, in seven phases, went on until 9.40, over a million shells being fired off, firstly against the artillery and finally on the front lines, against which 2,500 trench mortars were fired. An especially irritating gas was used, which caused some of the defenders to tear off their gas masks to scratch the itch, whereupon one or other of the poison gases took effect. The British rear areas were shattered, communications breaking down, and Gough, commanding the Fifth Army, lost control, as Capello had done at Caporetto, though his northern neighbour, Byng of the Third Army, held the bastion at Arras, to finally decisive effect. On the southern side, at La Fère and St Quentin, there was an exceptionally rapid advance: in a week, the Germans advanced forty miles on a fifty-mile front. They inflicted 300,000 casualties, and the tactics of fast-moving infiltration meant that one third of these were prisoners. The British lost 1,300 guns.

They retreated back over the old Somme battlefield, and fell back on Amiens, the essential railway junction, distinguished by a cathedral that is the most accomplished, in terms of mathematics, of all the great French cathedrals. It was an extraordinary success for Germany, because mobility had been restored to the western front, such as had not been seen since 1914, when it had still been possible for cavalry to canter grandly over open fields. Now, the twentieth century had happened: there were immense advances in technology of all sorts, and Germany was leading the field. The success was such that Ludendorff himself lost any sense of perspective, forgot the lessons of Caporetto, and took his foot off the brake – a German weakness. He forgot that, however victorious an army, it would lose steam as it advanced. He sent troops in, first to the left, to reinforce the success, on the St Quentin–La Fère side – and then thought that he should perhaps try to take Arras on the other wing. But the troops were only able to carry light weaponry and the guns could not be easily dragged over the mud of the old Somme. The German offensive ended up with a ridge just short of the railway junction at Amiens, from which, with very careful firing, the heaviest German guns could reach the station, but only just. And then the rules of this war re-asserted themselves: the importance of reserves, in this case brought up by a British classic, the red, double-decker London bus. Besides, German troops, falling upon masses of British stores, gorged themselves in a way unthinkable behind their own lines.

There were two great differences from Caporetto, other than mountainous terrain. In the first place, as mentioned, German guns could not be easily hauled over the slough of despond of the old Somme battlefields, whatever Porsche's engineering genius; quite apart from the shortage of petrol, there was a near-absence of rubber, such that wooden or iron tyres were used for lorries, and these churned up the roads. Secondly, the Cadorna factor – preposterous obstinacy in error, and preposterous blaming of everyone else – did not come into play. The British infantry were at last well-served by their commander, who now did what he should have done before, and accepted a French commander, who would have charge of the reserves. On 26 March, at Doullens, he put himself under Foch, who, unlike so many other generals, learned instead of just repeating himself. He had in reality learned vastly since his days on the Marne, and he had a genius for making himself trusted by all parties. He controlled the reserves and thereby could dictate the strategy, which, with tact, he now did. By London bus, by lorry, by railway, twelve French divisions and some of the British reserve from Flanders came to the Amiens lines. There was no muddled retreat in different directions (as had happened at Gorlice in 1915 and at Caporetto), and by 4 April the German offensive was called off.

But Ludendorff's main idea was to clear the British from Flanders and capture the Channel ports – expelling the British from the Europe that Brest-Litovsk implied. The March offensive had drawn in forty-eight of the fifty-six British divisions, together with forty French ones, and Haig had only a single division in reserve. At Ypres, the British were in a very vulnerable position, and could be fired upon from three sides – a position that they had worsened for themselves by taking Passchendaele, part of a ridge at the tip of their salient. The German trains rolled again, and those thousands of guns were transferred. The aircraft identified British gun positions, and the guns fired against map references, without giving any indication beforehand that they even existed on the ground. At least the British had had the sense to abandon their thin salient at Passchendaele, but, even so, they were stretched too thinly on ground that reasons of prestige and propaganda forbade them to give up. On 9 April, two German armies attacked, again with the methods of 21 March, and again with the luck of very favourable weather. On the southern side, they struck at two divisions of Portuguese. They, like the Italians, were being made to run so as to learn to walk, or even to toddle. Their men were therefore used as cannon-fodder to get British support for the maintenance of the Portuguese empire in Africa. They were not enthusiastic. They broke. In the Ypres salient, defence in depth could not be organized in any event, given that the whole thing bulged out into German-held territory. There was another notable German victory. On 12 April the Germans not only took back the Messines ridge but, later, went on to seize a continuation of it, Mount Kemmel, the highest point all around. This was the moment at which the British were threatened by collapse, and Haig responded: he told his men the truth – 'backs to the wall' – and from then on displayed qualities (not least, an ability to learn) that come as a surprise. But he was helped by Ludendorff, success having gone to his head. He repeated his mistake of 21 March, and kept on. Then he ran into reserves brought up by bus and rail – in this case, twelve French divisions. The railway lines at Hazebrouck and Béthune remained in British hands, the Germans arriving over shattered countryside on foot, and exhausted in attacks over what was now marshy country on the river Lys (which gave its name to the battle). The Allies had lost 150,000, the Germans 110,000 (to which the quarter-million of the March offensive should be added) and these were losses that the Allies could afford, the Germans not.

There followed a long pause. The last conscription-year of Germany was being called up early, as the schoolboys took their final exams. There were also prisoners of war, returning from Russia, and Austria-Hungary was prevailed upon to send some men (they arrived without boots at Metz). The ranks were refilled, and the munitions production of the Hindenburg programme was still considerable, although there were signs of over-heating. Ludendorff's idea was still to take the Channel ports and disrupt the arrival of Anglo-American troops, but he needed to drain off the reserves that had been built up in that region since the Lys battle. He opted for a stroke against the French front north-east of Paris, on the Aisne, at the Chemin des Dames, and was again lucky. The French commander was one Duchêne, a man of singular inability to learn. He placed most of his men in the front positions, where they were most vulnerable to bombardment, and there were also five British divisions that had been withdrawn because they had had a very bad time in the March offensive and needed to rest in what was supposed to be a quiet area. The noise of

German movements was concealed by, of all things, the croaking of frogs in the Aisne, and the surprise was almost complete. On 27 May, 5,300 guns opened up, against 1,400, and two million shells were fired off in four hours, with the usual favourable weather.

The German Seventh Army (Hans von Böhn) then performed a near-miracle of advance, scaling almost vertical ridges, crossing the river Aisne to capture bridges intact, and even struggling across marsh. They reached the river Marne, from where a heavy gun, 'Big Bertha' (named after the wife of the arms-manufacturer, Krupp), sent shells to Paris, forty miles away. Then Ludendorff once again repeated his mistake of 21 March and 9 April. He went on, and on. German troops with light weaponry were taking on Allied reserves arriving, with heavy weaponry, by rail – thirty French reserve divisions. There were also now the Americans, who at Château Thierry and Belleau Wood had their first experience of European war, and acquitted themselves well. On 2 June a Franco-American counter-attack by twenty-seven divisions held the Marne line, and a German attack at Montdidier on 9 June, on the northern side of this battlefield and adjoining the old British Somme lines, failed. It was a sign of what was to come. Ludendorff's attacks had created three very large salients – extended lines, some of them sketchy, in open country, and open to attack – and the active front had been extended from 390 to 510 kilometres, while the German troops, buoyed up for all-out victory, were necessarily cast down by the failure of the Allies to collapse. And 200,000 Americans were arriving every month – a fact of which Allied propaganda made much.

The most vulnerable of Ludendorff's great salients was that created in the Marne battle, and its edges were marked by Soissons to the north-west, and Rheims to the south-east. Here, on 15 July, the last German offensive occurred. The Kaiser himself appeared, and the affair was billed as an imperial battle, or even as *Friedenssturm*, 'peace assault'. Fifty-two divisions were mustered, and the usual crushing artillery. However, the Allies now knew what to expect (and French intelligence worked very well, advertisements in the Luxemburg German-language press being used to convey messages detailing German railway movements). They also understood that the way to deal with Ludendorff's methods was counter-battery fire – that is, to conceal gun positions, and then to open up on the enemy artillery in mid-bombardment, once its positions had been made clear. East of Rheims, defence in depth meant that the Germans were tired out before they reached the main French positions. Pétain used his reserves, and the Germans were halted on 17 July.

Now came the riposte – a counter-attack on the other side of the salient, from the forest of Villers-Cotterêts (the birthplace of Alexandre Dumas). The French had developed a light and fast-moving tank. Two generals, Debeney on the British right, and Mangin, to his right, began the tactics that were to become famous in 1940 as *Blitzkrieg* – tanks, fast-moving infantry, and aircraft flying low to keep the German gunners' heads down.

Three hundred tanks (Renault) and eighteen divisions, two of them American, struck in open cornfield, entirely by surprise, and went five miles forward. With the whole of the German force in the Marne salient threatened by a cut-off, Ludendorff pulled back from it, back to the Chemin des Dames. By 4 August the French had taken 30,000 prisoners and 600 guns. Foch then discovered how this war was to be won: he stopped. No more battering with light weapons against reserves. The answer was to suspend the attack where it had succeeded, and attack somewhere else, keeping the enemy reserves on the move. Move, they did: demoralizing slow journeys by train, halts, countermandings, continuations, and all of it in hot weather.

German reserves were now being badly disrupted – in fact a third of the entire German army was to spend the last three months of the war in or near slow-moving trains. Ludendorff had been setting everything up for a great Flanders attack. Now he had to put it off again and again. His defence expert, Lossberg, wished to withdraw, even to the Meuse and Antwerp, but Ludendorff overruled him. The French maintained some pressure in the Chemin des Dames, but the next main Allied action was British, at Amiens, on 8 August. Here was a limited scheme, simply to push the Germans back out of range of the station, and the French example of 18 July was properly studied. The generals – Rawlinson on the British side, Monash and Currie on the Australian and Canadian – were eminently practical men who were able to persuade Haig, when the time came, not to persist with the attack beyond a few days. Air control was established, and there was now a great profusion of weaponry of all types, particularly light Lewis guns that could be carried by fast-moving infantry. The noise of tanks coming into line was masked by aircraft flying low, back and forth. There was no preliminary bombardment at all, and morning mist concealed the initial attack. The new Mark V and Whippet tanks were much faster and more reliable than earlier ones, and a special development was the laying down of a curtain of gas and high explosive in the German rear areas, to disrupt any counter-attack. The result, on 8 August, was a triumph, the Germans taken by surprise, in almost open-country positions that had not been thoroughly prepared; a brigade staff was captured at breakfast. On the first day, 12,000 prisoners and 400 guns were captured; almost 50,000 prisoners were taken by the end of the operation.

There is a mysterious process in the defeat of any army – the point at which the men give up hope. In the Russian case, the point was reached towards the end of the Brusilov offensive in September 1916, with the endless bloody failures of the Guard Army in the marshes before Kovel and Vladimir Volynsk. The German army's morale began to break on 18 July, when the Villers-Cotterêts counter-attack was under way. The Kaiser, at the headquarters town of Spa, in Belgium, politely asked Ludendorff what had gone wrong, and Ludendorff said that the men were just not fighting any more – thousands were surrendering. A further sign was that men were reporting sick in greater and greater numbers. Curiously enough, if troops are well-led, they do not fall ill: before Trafalgar, in 1805, the French admiral had to leave 1,000 men behind in the West Indies, whereas the British admiral, Lord Nelson, lost no one in precisely the same area.[2] Ludendorff even allowed himself a note of reproach towards the Kaiser. His own belief (like Cadorna's) was that the political Left were being allowed to spread defeatism. But now, after Amiens, it was Ludendorff's own nerves that began to crack. He began to hit the bottle and provoked quarrels with his subordinates – even with poor old Hindenburg, who had been doing no one any harm and looked the very part of fatherly commander-in-chief; he even wrote to his wife, before the offensive had started, to the effect that the general staff were very busy, that he would have time on his hands, and could he be sent the various German classics to be re-read? Now, Ludendorff was saying that he could only manage a defensive action. Foch showed him to be accurate.

Foch kept up the pressure, arguing in a clever memorandum that the key was to stop after the initial successes. The British army took the lead in these – Arras on 17 August, Bapaume in the Somme country on the 21st, an outrunner of the great Siegfried line called the Drocourt-Quéant switch on the 26th, St Quentin on the 28th, Mount Kemmel on 4 September. Meanwhile, the French re-took the entire salient created by the German success of 27 May, and on 12 September came a major American effort, in which half a million troops with 1,500 aircraft and 270 light tanks cleared the St Mihiel salient to the south-east of Verdun (though the Germans managed to withdraw most of their men in time). Then came a brief hold-up at Ypres, and, towards the end of the month, the Americans showed that they did not have much to learn from the British when it came to making mistakes and persisting in them. In the Argonne country north of Verdun, much of it devastated and studded with rivers and ravines that made use of tanks impossible, fifteen (double-sized) American and twenty-two French divisions went into operation with an eight-to-one superiority. But there was a logistical breakdown, and American commanders persisted in neglecting the tactical lessons of 1917: they used old-fashioned methods, and wasted much of the training time on rifle fire, itself now becoming almost obsolete. Then they ran into a prepared position, the Kriemhild line, and stuck – the one real advantage being that German reserves (thirty-six divisions) had had to be concentrated there.

This enabled the British to stage what was to be almost a model battle and to crack the Siegfried line (referred to by the British as the 'Hindenburg line'). On 27 September an enormous force assaulted nine miles of it, before Cambrai. The defences were three miles thick, and a special feature was that they included the St Quentin canal, which had fifty feet of sloping banks down to its six-foot depth of muddy water. The only way across for tanks seemed to be a great tunnel, through which the canal passed, but it was thickly covered with wire, and the tanks were held up. However, there was a prodigious bombardment, with 126 shells from the field guns alone landing every minute on 500 yards of trench, over an eight-hour period, and the counter-battery fire by the heavy artillery had been very well prepared, silencing the German heavy artillery. The defenders were in effect stunned. An element of luck supervened, in that the British had captured outline maps of the defences, and there was further luck at the canal, with fog, which allowed a single division to cross, clamber up the opposite bank, and breach the Siegfried line on a three-mile front. This feat of arms enabled Australians and Canadians on either side to move forward, and by 5 October the British were into open country. Haig again proposed to stop, but the German retreat went on, leaving the front early in November just short of Brussels and Namur. In mid October the Americans at last broke through the Kriemhild line, and could threaten the great German railway base of Metz.

It was obvious enough that Germany would be defeated. She had lost over a million men between March and July, and a further three quarters of a million in the succeeding months, half of them made prisoner. There was also a crisis in the war economy, with plant wearing down, and the Social Democrat leader complained that working-class north and east Berlin lacked the 4,000 railway-wagons used for transportation of the vital potatoes. No doubt the country could have fought on, into 1919, as it did in 1945, but the end was in sight. On 28 September Ludendorff's nerves cracked, and he raged against everyone, including in the end the Kaiser: the war would have to be stopped. 'No confidence can be placed in the troops,' he told his staff. Of course, the army could have made a stand on the river Rhine, but everything was falling apart, and Germany's allies now dropped out. They had all been following events in the west and, with the failure of Ludendorff's great offensive, were looking to save what they could from the overall wreckage.

On 15 September the Allied force at Salonica, which had at last ceased to be what the Germans contemptuously called their greatest prisoner-of-war camp, moved forward, and the Bulgarians collapsed. They had not, anyway, been rewarded by the Germans as they had expected – no southern Balkan empire, as in days of (long-ago) yore. On the 28th they asked for an armistice. That cut the link to the Ottoman empire, but in any case the Young Turks were also angry at German interference in the Caucasus, and some were wondering whether they might not abandon the Germans and leave the Arabs to the British, while concentrating, with British support, on the Caucasus and its oil. Enver Pasha was thinking through the alternative to the Ottoman empire – a national Turkey which would take over Turkic Central Asia. The Young Turks left on a German submarine, to Odessa, and went their ways – Afghanistan, the Caucasus, Berlin, Moscow – to set this up. The Ottoman army withdrew from Syria, and an armistice was arranged on 30 October. Then the Austrians dropped out. Before then the Austro-Hungarian government had made noises about the acceptance of President Wilson's 'Fourteen Points', and the Emperor appointed as prime minister a professor, Lammasch, who even believed in them (he ended, in exile, as a professor at Berkeley). But it was the end of the Habsburg empire. Hungary declared independence; so did national councils representing the various other non-German peoples. The Germans of Austria, curiously enough, were first in the queue: they expected to join Germany. At that, there was even a brief German invasion of Austria. The Italians took advantage of the confusion to round up hundreds of thousands of unresisting soldiers in the last days of October and called it the battle of Vittorio Veneto.

Germany still had some cards. True, the army was not what it had been, but elements of it were still formidable. She ran large parts of Russia and Turkey. Winter was coming up. The Rhine was an obstacle, and war-weariness was a considerable factor on the Allied side. So, too, was potential disagreement: would the British, with their empire, be happy with President Wilson's Fourteen Points, which included provisions for the emancipation of colonies? After all, Brest-Litovsk had meant self-determination for the non-Russian peoples of the Tsarist empire, and there was the further possibility that an appeal could be made for Germany to be kept going as the leading anti-Communist state. Ludendorff now had a puppet foreign secretary, and, late in September, after the Bulgarian armistice, he cobbled together a plan, not revealed to the Chancellor. President Wilson could be appealed to, and that would mean formally making Germany more democratically run. The German Left might as well make itself useful as a stage-prop in this sense. Ludendorff, and many other national-ists, were already blaming it for the drop in morale, for the disorders of the economy and for the inflation caused by high wages. On 30 September a new chancellor was appointed, Prince Max of Baden, a liberal-minded south German, and his cabinet included representatives of the Centre and Left parties. Prince Max did understand that, if he asked for an armistice, it might just break the morale of the people irretrievably: they would realize that that was that, and there might be a sudden collapse, which would leave no room for negotiations. He was, as it happens, right. The Kaiser made his last calamitous contribution to German history when he sniffed that, 'You have not been appointed to make difficulties for the High Command,' and a public note was sent to the United States in the night of 4–5 October. Ludendorff was really saving his own reputation: he would encour-age others to make an end to the war, then turn round and say it had not been his fault.

At the end of the film *Oh! What a Lovely War* there is a scene of genius, as war graves, stretching all over the screen, have red tape slowly wound round them. This was what now happened. Officials and High Commands solemnly debated the ins and outs of the armistice for rather more than a month, and meanwhile the men went on fighting and dying, in tens of thousands. The German Note gave the Allies some trouble, because they were being forced to talk the language of democracy and self-determination whereas they were all resolved on vengeance and the creation of empires at the expense of the defeated. Even the Belgians thought that they should seize the Scheldt estuary from the Dutch. Getting a unified response, combining rapacity with sanctity, was difficult, though in the end British skills prevailed.

The Germans themselves were clumsy. The leaders of the Centre and Left – Matthias Erzberger and Philipp Scheidemann – sensibly wanted to adopt the Fourteen Points, but the generals only even looked at them on 5 October and the foreign office thought that they might be useful negotiation points and no more. The notes went back and forth – Wilson on the 8th, Berlin on the 12th, Wilson on the 14th, Berlin on the 20th, and then another exchange by the end of the month. Perhaps, if the Germans had been more realistic, something could have been saved. But they persisted with illusion, and on 12 October committed the blunder of sinking a British passenger liner, *Leinster*, drowning 450 people, including 135 women and children; in their retreat through Flanders, they were poisoning wells and 'ringing' fruit-trees. If Wilson began with hints of magnanimity, alarming his Allies, his demands now went up. Germany was to have proper democracy, a constitutional monarchy, and the submarines were to stop. Prince Max accepted. At this point, Ludendorff altogether reversed his original line, and started manufacturing a very dangerous legend – that Germany had not really lost. He came to Berlin, without the Kaiser's say-so, and said that Germany could fight on. On 26 October he denounced the terms being announced by his own nominees in the foreign office, and had a row with the Kaiser, whom he insulted; of Prince Max and his well-meaning left-wing associates he remarked, 'these people can ingest the soup that they have brewed up for us.' They did. The army leaders preserved their prestige intact. In due course, Ludendorff used his own to introduce Adolf Hitler into German politics,[3] and, ten years later, in 1933, old Hindenburg, as president, appointed him chancellor.

Meanwhile, as German morale was collapsing, the final crisis was precipitated by another act of desperation. In a weird descant upon the navy–army rivalry that had done so much to weaken the war effort, the naval authorities resolved on a last, mad move. Captain von Levetzow, chief of staff of the navy, could see the likelihood that Germany's great ships would be interned, none of them left for the eventual reconstitution of the *Reichsmarine*. Better, he thought, 'immortal fame at the bottom of the ocean', and orders went out on 27 October for the High Seas Fleet to put to sea in the general direction of the Thames Estuary. The 80,000 sailors and stokers were not enthusiastic about the bottom of the ocean. They mutinied at Kiel, then at Lübeck and Wilhelmshaven, and insurrection spread to Cologne, then Munich, where an actor took over. There was now an air of Russia, with workers' and soldiers' councils being formed. The Social Democrats, already in government under Prince Max, knew that, if they were to avoid a Bolshevik revolution, certain things would have to be done. The war would have to be stopped forthwith and the Kaiser would have to go. The generals told him as much, and on 9 November he abdicated (escaping to Holland) just as the republic was being declared in Berlin. In any case, with the country in chaos, the time had come for an immediate armistice. A deputation made its way to Foch's headquarters in the forest of Compiègne, and the guns stopped at 11 a.m. on 11 November. The terms were harsh: Germany would not be able to fight again. The Allies took the Rhine. There was no occupation of Germany – as things turned out, a fatal decision. But it was over.

NOTES

1. W. Baumgart, *Deutsche Ostpolitik 1918* (Vienna, 1918), p. 174 ff. notes the importance of oil.
2. R. Atkinson, *Trafalgar* (London, 2004), pp. 40 ff. – an extraordinarily erudite disquisition on medicine at that time.
3. In 1923 he led an attempt at a coup in Munich, together with Hitler, whom he made respectable. In the 1930s he was, however, the only public opponent of the Third Reich (he thought it was inadequately anti-Catholic) until someone noticed what he was writing. He had a state funeral in 1938, at which mourners wore weird helmets and made strange moan.

preceding pages: Returning German army marching through Berlin, December 1918

President Wilson himself arrived in Europe (to tremendous enthusiasm) in mid December, and represented a sort of new world order, in which Progress and Freedom could resume the forward march that had stopped in 1914. Peace treaties were sorted out – more by haggling among the Allies than with the defeated states, which were just told to sign on the dotted line – in various palaces in the Paris region. The chief treaty was concluded at Versailles, with the Germans on 28 June 1919, others following. In the famous painting by Sir William Orpen, the peace-makers look extraordinarily pleased with themselves as they pose, in Louis XIV's Hall of Mirrors, for rather wooden immortalization: silkiness of moustache, acuteness of gaze, dignity of stance. A Maharajah and a Japanese baron look on, evidence of the peace-makers' internationalism and benevolence. Clemenceau is said to have remarked that he was sitting between a would-be Napoleon (Lloyd George) and a would-be Jesus Christ (Wilson).

Even at the time there was not much reason for these

people's self-confidence. A worldwide epidemic of influenza carried off ten million victims; civil war carried off more millions in Russia, until, in 1920, the Bolsheviks won. The Allies' attempt to divide up the Middle East soon came to grief. Muslim Arab countries – and their oil supplies – were mainly taken over by the British, and their expert on the area, T. E. Lawrence, remarked with wonder that whereas the Turks had run Iraq with a locally raised army of 14,000 men, executing ninety people a year, the British, with 100,000 soldiers, tanks, aircraft and gas, faced a war with everybody. The Sultan, prisoner of the British and French occupying Istanbul, was forced in 1920 to sign a treaty at Sèvres that not only vastly truncated his realm, but subjected it to a process of forced re-civilization.[1] Greeks and Armenians invaded Anatolia, with the blessing of the British and French. The Turks, uniquely among the defeated powers, recovered, under a leader of genius, and in 1922 re-took their country: at Lausanne in 1923 it was then recognized. Paradoxically, it is the only creation of the post-war period that has flourished ever since: the rest came to grief, in some cases quite quickly, and those beautifully tailored statesmen in the Orpen portrait were in most cases repudiated by their own voters. Their creations went sour. In 1919, the European empires were greatly extended. Within ten years, these empires were falling apart and within a generation were finished.

The list of the failures of Versailles goes on and on. A 'League of Nations' was set up, to adjudicate international problems. It began quite well by organizing population-transfers in the Balkans. Then, confronted with major matters, it declined into irrelevance, greeting the outbreak of the Second World War with a debate about the standardization of level-crossings. The attempt to put the world's economy together also came to grief. By 1920, the post-war boom had fizzled out, and by 1929 the greatest economic crisis in the history of the world had arrived, bringing with it political disasters all over. The would-be parliamentary nation-states established in 1918–19 generally ceased to be parliamentary, and Bolshevik Russia, which in the 1920s had something of a human face, acquired, under Stalin, a monstrous one.

The worst problem by far concerned Germany. In February 1919, meeting in Weimar, the new republican politicians devised a democratic constitution, perhaps the most literal-mindedly democratic constitution ever (so determined were its makers to show proper Wilsonian credentials that they provided for relentless elections and proportional voting). At Versailles, there were territorial losses, particularly to Poland, which were quite widely resented. But the real problem was money. 'The Germans' were formally blamed for the war, and were expected to pay 'reparations' for the damage they had caused. But the French really meant to use this device to prevent the German economy from recovering, and other former Allies expected to pay off their war-debts. In 1921, the sum of 132,000,000,000 gold Marks was arrived at, which meant that, annually, Germany would be handing over for generations a quarter of the money she earned from exports. Such sums might be extracted from an occupied country, as the Nazis displayed in France during the Second World War and as the European Economic Community did in Germany thereafter. The Allies had deliberately avoided occupying Germany, for fear of the upheavals that might result; they therefore expected democratic politicians to cooperate with them. It was asking too much. In the 1920s, American investment went into Germany, and was used to pay the annual reparations charge. Then the world economy broke down, and the American money ceased to flow. More or less all Germans blamed their economic plight on reparations, more generally on Versailles, and this was Hitler's strongest card. In fact, Weimar democracy broke down in 1930, in the sense that there was no longer a parliamentary majority prepared to take responsibility; the largest political party, the Social Democrats, distinguished itself by 'constructive abstention' – meaning that it would vote neither for nor against – and the *Reichstag* kept dissolving itself: in 1932 there were more election-days than there were parliamentary sessions, and the aged president, Hindenburg, ruled by decree. In 1933, a majority of German voters were either Communist or Nazi, and Hitler was appointed chancellor. He appealed for full powers, in other words dictatorship, and needed a two thirds majority in the *Reichstag* for this. He got it, and the final surreal note to the post-war settlement was supplied by the guiding light of the Weimar Republic, the Democrats. By then they (under a different name) were down to five seats. When it came to Hitler's vote, they divided. Two deputies voted for Hitler, two against, and the other abstained, protesting that the others were splitting the party. By then, reparations had been abolished, but the damage had been done, and Hitler embarked on an extreme-nationalist programme.

The real disaster, in all of this, was that Germans did not think that they had been defeated. They had, as the legend was to have it, been 'stabbed in the back': Jews, the Left, soft-brained academics had prevented them from winning the war and setting up a Europe that had more sense, on the ground, than anything dreamed up by the naive Americans. Ludendorff was the main architect of this fantasy, but even then by accident: a British journalist asked him in English whether he felt that Germany had been 'stabbed in the back', and, upon translation, Ludendorff said yes.

The disaster that followed had been sensed by Lloyd George, in the last days of the First World War, when armistice terms were being discussed. He made a prophetic remark: 'if peace were made now, in twenty years' time the Germans would say what Carthage had said about the First Punic War, namely that they had made this mistake and that mistake, and by better preparation and organization they would be able to bring about victory next time.'[2] This was more or less what Hitler said in *Mein Kampf* – Germany deserved to have won, and would have done so if only it had not been for treachery, out-of-place humanitarian nonsense, and all the appeasement of traitors on the Left. On 10 November, he was convalescing from gassing, which had blinded him, and when he heard someone saying that a revolution had broken out, he reacted: 'since the day when I had stood at my mother's grave I had not wept . . . It had all been in vain . . . Did all this happen so that a gang of wretched criminals could lay hands on the fatherland? The more I tried to achieve clarity on the monstrous event in this hour, the more the shame of indignation and disgrace burned my brow. What was all the pain in my eyes compared to this misery?' The conclusion that he drew was that 'there is no making pacts with Jews. There can only be the hard: either, or.' The way was open for a Second World War even more terrible than the First.

NOTES

1. One clause of the treaty (never ratified) was that the sale of dirty postcards would be suppressed (Murat Bardakci, *Sahbaba* (Istanbul, 1998) p. 163).

2. John Grigg, *Lloyd George: War Leader* (London, 2001) is a most sympathetic book, in both senses, and it is a great misfortune that the author did not live to complete the story, the unravelling of Lloyd George's plans after victory.

Europe in 1914

NORWAY

N

North
Sea

DENMARK

Copenhagen

BRITAIN

Dublin

The
Hague   Elbe
London   Berlin
NETHERLANDS   Potsdam
Thames   Brussels
English Channel   Liège   GERMAN
BELG.
LUXEMBURG

ATLANTIC

Seine
OCEAN   Marne   Rhine   Danube
Paris

Loire   Berne
SWITZERLAND

FRANCE   Po

Adria

PORTUGAL

Madrid   Rome

Lisbon   SPAIN   ITALY

Mediterranean Sea

SPAN. MOROCCO.
ALGERIA   TUNISIA
MOROCCO   (France)   (France)
(France)

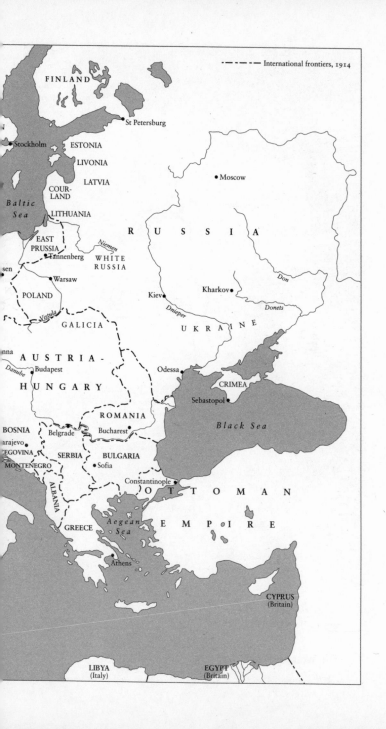

FINLAND

St Petersburg

Stockholm

ESTONIA

LIVONIA

LATVIA

COUR-
LAND

*Baltic
Sea*

LITHUANIA

Moscow

R   U   S   S   I   A

EAST
PRUSSIA

Niemen

Tannenberg

WHITE
RUSSIA

sen

Warsaw

Kharkov

Don

POLAND

Vistula

GALICIA

Kiev

Dnieper

Donets

U K R A I N E

nna

AUSTRIA-

Danube   Budapest

HUNGARY

Odessa

CRIMEA

Sebastopol

ROMANIA

Black Sea

BOSNIA

Belgrade

Bucharest

arajevo

EGOVINA

SERBIA

BULGARIA

MONTENEGRO

Sofia

Constantinople

O   T   T   O   M   A   N

ALBANIA

GREECE

*Aegean
Sea*

E   M   P   I   R   E

Athens

CYPRUS
(Britain)

LIBYA
(Italy)

EGYPT
(Britain)

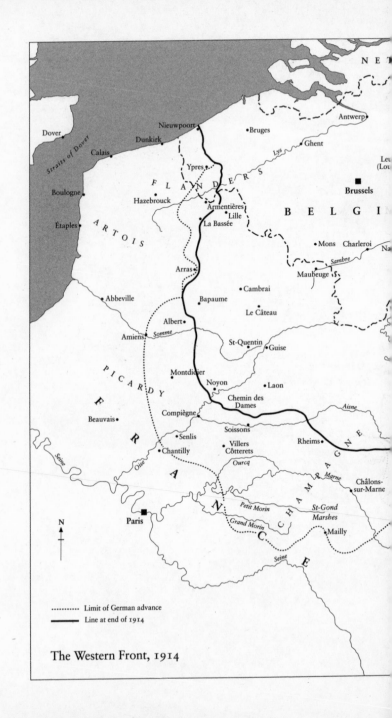

The Western Front, 1914

········· Limit of German advance
——— Line at end of 1914

RLANDS

Maastricht
Liège
Spa
Meuse

ARDENNES   LUXEMBURG

Luxemburg
Moselle
Longwy
Briey
Thionville
Verdun
Woëvre
Metz
SAAR
St-Mihiel
Morhange
LORRAINE
Toul   Nancy
Sarrebourg

GERMANY

Vosges Mts

Rhine

Strasbourg

ALSACE

Colmar

The Ypres Salient, 1914–1918

Houlthulst
Forest

Roulers

Langemarck
*Front Line
Nov. 6, 1917*
*Front Line
Nov. 22, 1914*

Pilckem
Ridge
Passchendaele

*Front Line
Nov. 14, 1917*
Broodseinde

Steenbeek

Polygon Wood

Ypres   Hooge

BELGIUM

*Front Line
April 30, 1918*
Gheluvelt

Canal

*Front Line
June 7, 1917*
Menin Road
Menin

Wytschaete
Messines
Comines

Warneton
Lys

FRANCE

0   miles

Armentières

NETHERLANDS
Aachen

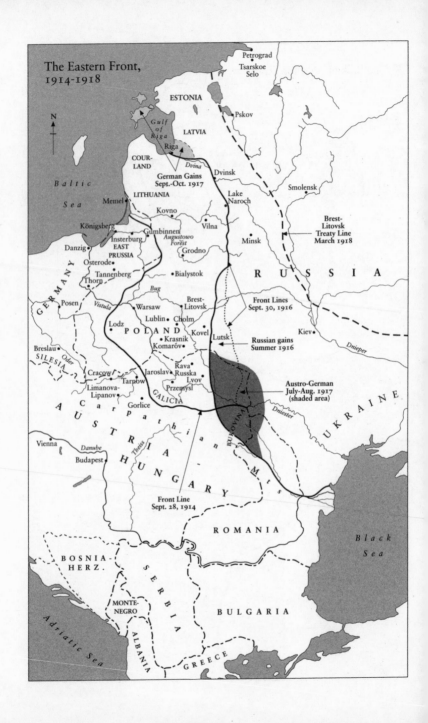

The Eastern Front, 1914-1918

The Balkans and the Straits

N

RUSSIA

Vienna

Danube

Budapest

AUSTRIA-HUNGARY

Dniester

Jassy

BESSARABIA

Pruth

Odessa

TRANSYLVANIA

Temesvar

Sava

Focşani

CROATIA

Belgrade

Ploesti

BOSNIA-HERZ.

Cer △

Morava

Kolubara

ROMANIA

Bucharest

DOBRUDJA

Constantza

Black Sea

Sarajevo

Nish

S E R B I A

Sofia

Danube

MONTE-NEGRO

BULGARIA

Adriatic Sea

Cetinje

Scutari

ALBANIA

KOSOVO

Vardar

Bosphorus

Constantinople

ITALY

Monastir

MACEDONIA

Salonica

Sea of Marmora

O T T O M A N

Straits of Otranto

Valona

GREECE

Lemnos

Aegean Sea

E M P I R E

Corfu

Izmir (Smyrna)

Athens

Mediterranean Sea

The Dardanelles 1915

Maximum Allied occupation August 1915

Aegean Sea

Suvla Bay

Anzac Cove

GALLIPOLI

Chanak

DARDANELLES

Achi Baba

Krithia

Cape Helles

Salonika Front Line in November 1916

Salonika Front Line at the end of September 1918

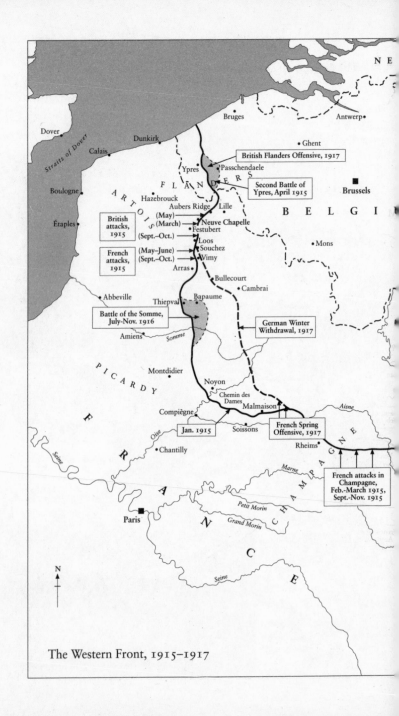

The Western Front, 1915–1917

ERLANDS

R U H R

•Düsseldorf

Cologne•

•Aachen

Liège

Meuse

G E R M A N Y

Koblenz

Frankfurt•

•Mainz

Bad Kreuznach•

RDENNES   LUXEMBURG   *Moselle*

an

Luxemburg

Longwy

attle of Verdun
eb.–Aug. 1916

Briey•

Fort Douaumont

Thionville

Verdun

Fort Vaux

Woëvre

Metz•

St-
Mihiel

rench attack
April 1915

Toul•   •Nancy

S A A R

L O R R A I N E

V o s g e s   M t s

Rhine

Strasbourg•

A L S A C E

Colmar•

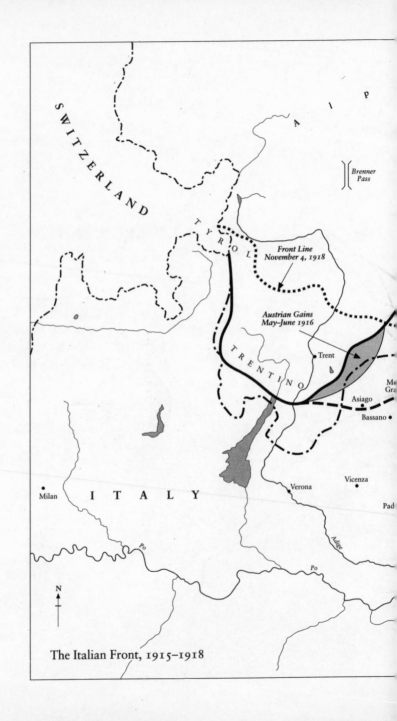

The Italian Front, 1915–1918

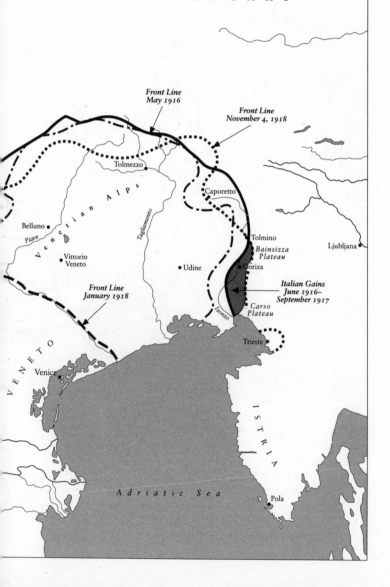

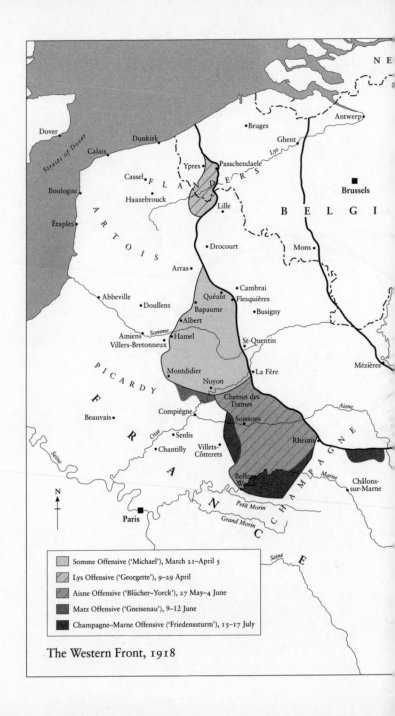

The Western Front, 1918

Legend:

- Somme Offensive ('Michael'), March 21–April 5
- Lys Offensive ('Georgette'), 9–29 April
- Aisne Offensive ('Blücher–Yorck'), 27 May–4 June
- Matz Offensive ('Gneisenau'), 9–12 June
- Champagne–Marne Offensive ('Friedensturm'), 15–17 July

Some Sources

This list partly reproduces my own sources, but is mainly designed to cite the literature produced in the last few years, of which there has been much. Older works will be found in *their* bibliographies, and only in rare – very rare – cases do I mention them (sometimes with the most recent date of reprint). One of these is my own, *The Eastern Front 1914–1917* (London 1975) – still, apparently, the main work on the matter: the Russians should have made it obsolete a long time ago. All other countries, including Turkey, are far ahead in publications.

The three most recent large-scale accounts of the First World War are especially useful because they bring earlier ones up to date with the prodigious amount of work that has been done in recent times. David Stevenson, *1914–1918: The History of the First World War* (Penguin, 2004) is extraordinarily informative on all matters, for instance the progress made by medicine or aircraft. Niall Ferguson, *The Pity of War* (Penguin, 1998) is equally far-ranging, though in a different way:

it is particularly interesting on war finance, a vastly important subject, but has much of importance to say on other matters – for instance soldiers' morale and why they fought as they did. Hew Strachan, *The First World War*, Vol. I: *To Arms* (Oxford, 2001) is the first of three proposed volumes, and the author knows the military inside-out: he also covers the first months of the Ottoman war effort. I have owed much to all three of these books.

There are several other shorter accounts, each with its strong point. Robin Prior and Trevor Wilson, *The First World War* (Cassell, 2001) is very useful on military technicalities, for instance the changes in artillery usage that occurred. They are not respectful of A. J. P. Taylor's short *The First World War* (1966, but endlessly re-printed by Penguin). I am. For the eastern front, I am told in Moscow that an official history will at last appear in 2014. Italy is well covered – excellent photographs and a solid bibliographical discussion – in Mario Isnenghi and Giorgio Rochat, *La Grande Guerra 1914–1918* (Milan, 2004), Austria-Hungary by Manfred Rauchensteiner, *Der Tod des Doppeladlers* (Graz, 1993); the most recent work on France is Anthony Clayton, *Paths of Glory: The French Army 1914–1918* (London, 2005), though see also J.-B. Duroselle, *La Grande Guerre des Français* (Paris, 1994). The Turkish front is covered by Edward J. Erickson, *Ordered to Die* (Westport, Conn., 2000) but see also Michael Carver, *The Turkish Front* (London, 2001), though Commandant Larcher, *La Guerre turque dans la guerre mondiale* (Paris, 1926) still needs to be read. For Germany, G. Hirschfeld (ed.), *Enzyklopädie Erster Weltkrieg* (Munich, 2003) is useful, and there are summaries of important matters, given that some of the documentation disappeared; see also Holger Herwig, *The First World War: Germany and Austria-Hungary 1914–1918* (London, 1997).

I have used these as the basis for my narrative. However, it is now easily possible to supplement the basic accounts with a vast amount of research on the internet. A Google search on any name or topic usually brings remarkable results, the more so as many museums have their own websites. The Imperial War Museum in London is representative, and remarkable (*www.iwm.org.uk*), but there are many private websites, such as *www.worldwar1.com*, *www.grande-guerre.org*, or *www.firstworldwar.com*, and I have traced many biographies through others, such as *www.findagrave.com*. There are equivalents in other countries, but the British – or at any rate the 'Anglo-Saxons' – are far in the lead.

As further reading (and sources) in connection with my own chapters, the following (complementary to the works mentioned above) may be cited:

Chapter 1: the most recent book is David Fromkin, *Europe's Last Summer: Who Started the War in 1914?* (New York, 2004), with a decent booklist. James Joll, *The Origins of the First World War* (Longman, 1992) still remains important, and, for the background, so does A. J. P. Taylor: *The Struggle for Mastery in Europe 1848–1918* (Oxford, 1954). It was written at a time when the crisis of July 1914 could still be seen as the outcome of a series of diplomatic crises, and these (Morocco etc.) are superbly covered, though Taylor was inclined to see July 1914 as a product of 'the system' rather than of plotting in Berlin. Imanuel Geiss, *Julikrise und Kriegsausbruch, 1914* (2 vols., Hanover, 1963–64), with an abridged English edition, *July 1914* (London, 1967), *did* document the outbreak of the war as a *mise-en-scène*, and further corroborative evidence, from papers that had escaped destruction, then began to emerge: see Angela Mombauer, *Origins of the First World War* (Harlow, 2002). Geiss subverted the important myth that Russian mobilization prompted Germany; see also V. Berghahn, *Germany and the Approach of War in 1914* (Basingstoke, 1995): his advantage is that he understands the dimension of the navy.

Chapter 2: on the opening round, L. Burchardt, *Friedenswirtschaft und Kriegsvorsorge* (Boppard, 1968) and L. J. Farrar, *The Short-war Illusion* (Santa Barbara, 1973) variously discuss this important matter. Winston Churchill's *World Crisis* (6 vols., London 1923–31) is wonderfully dramatic on the Marne, and so is John Keegan, *The First World War* (London 1998). D. E. Showalter, *Tannenberg* (Hamden, Conn., 1991) deserves mention.

Chapter 3: Tim Travers, *The Killing Ground* (Barnsley, 2003) is an important study of the British army's 'learning curve'. Robert Graves, *Goodbye to All That* (London, 1960) is a classic disillusioned account of the 'New Army' as it started off in France, and compare

Barry Webb, *Edmund Blunden* (London, 1990) for a more resigned view. Another classic British observer was E. L. Spears, liaison officer with the French (in both world wars), and his life is excellently recorded by Max Egremont, *Under Two Flags* (London, 1997). For Italian intervention, Indro Montanelli, *L'Italia di Giolitti* (Rizzoli, 1975) is wonderfully readable and given to the black humour that modern Italy sometimes brings out. On the Dardanelles campaign, Nigel Steel and Peter Hart, *Defeat at Gallipoli* (London, 2002) and Tim Travers, *Gallipoli 1915* (London, 2001) are solid and very fair-minded. On the Armenian issue, Guenter Lewy, *The Armenian Massacres in Ottoman Turkey* (Utah, 2005) replaces everything, but Franz Werfel's *Vierzig Tage des Musa Dagh,* originally written in 1932, woodenly translated into English, is a magnificent novel, taking some liberties with the history. Werfel wrote on his title page: *nicht gegen Tuerken polemisieren*, 'do not use this against the Turks'. If only. On the blockade, G.-H. Soutou, *L'Or et le sang* (Paris, 1989) discusses (predatory) Allied economic war aims, and A. Offer, *The First World War: An Agrarian Interpretation* (Oxford, 1989) puts them in an interesting and original perspective. Gerd Hardach, *The First World War* (London, 1977) came as part of a series of books on economic history and is still the widest survey of a gigantic subject (on the financial aspects of which Niall Ferguson, *op. cit.*, is the best introduction).

Chapter 4: on Verdun there is a classic: Alistair Horne, *The Price of Glory* (London, 1978). Holger

Afflerbach, *Falkenhayn* (Munich, 1996) corrects much of the legendry. On the Somme, the latest work is Peter Hart, *The Somme* (London, 2005). There is still much fighting over British strategy. John Terraine wrote a heroically unfashionable book in 1963, *Haig, the Educated Soldier*. It was the very moment when *Oh! What a Lovely War*, as a sort of musical based on the soldiers' songs, and then as a film, appeared in London (and Paris) – the film, and even more the stage version, amounting to genius. Terraine's defence has probably had the best of things, given the vast difficulties that Haig faced. Lyn Macdonald has done a wonderful job in collecting accounts of life in the trenches in each of the years of the First World War. Her *Somme* appeared in 1993. On Jutland, Arthur Marder, *From the Dreadnought to Scapa Flow: The Royal Navy in the Fisher Era* (5 vols., London 1961–70) is the established labour of love.

Chapter 5: the background to the Central Powers' peace offer is in Fritz Fischer, *Griff nach der Weltmacht*, translated (London, 1967) as *Germany's Aims in the First World War*. On American intervention Barbara Tuchman, *The Zimmermann Telegram* (London, 1966) is a very good introduction (she was the daughter of ambassador Morgenthau in Istanbul). The French disasters of spring 1917 are laid out in G. Pedroncini, *Les Mutineries de 1917* (Paris 1967). Prior and Wilson's *Passchendaele: The Untold Story* (Yale, 1996) is a model account of a battle on the western front; but Leon Wolff, *In Flanders Fields* (London, 1958) is devastating; I read it (together with Robert Graves) one Christmas in my teens, and have never forgotten either. There is a large literature on the Italian disaster: two British mountaineers, John and Eileen Wilks, wrote *Rommel and Caporetto* (Leo Cooper, 2001) with remarkable insight into terrain and sources alike; Mario Isnenghi, *I Vinti di Caporetto* (Milan, 1967) asked questions about morale, and his *Grande Guerra* (*op cit.*) contains a very thorough bibliography. Heinz von Lichem, *Krieg in den Alpen*, vol. 3 (Augsburg, 1993) is episodic and romantic, but also knows about mountains. On Russia in 1917, we have two very different but immensely thorough books: Richard Pipes, *The Russian Revolution* (London, 1999) and Orlando Figes, *A People's Tragedy* (London, 1997). How Lenin arrived at his intuitive judgements is well explained in Robert Service, *Lenin* (2 vols., Basingstoke, 1991). Russian historians are well represented by Oleg Airapetov, *Poslednyaya Voyna Imperatorskoy Rossii* (Moscow, 2002) and *Generaly, Liberaly i Predprinimately* (Moscow, 2003) which acutely examines the divisions at the top in Russia before the Revolution.

Chapter 6: J. W. Wheeler Bennett, *Brest-Litovsk: The Forgotten Peace* (London, 1938) is *the* book, but W. Baumgart, *Deutsche Ostpolitik 1918* (Vienna, 1966) has important details regarding the Caucasus, Ukraine, etc. The Ludendorff offensives are discussed in Martin Middlebrook, *The Kaiser's Battle* (London, 1978) and Tim Travers, *How the War was Won* (London, 1992); for the decline of the German war economy, see G. D. Feldman, *Army, Industry and Labour in Germany*

1914–1918 (Princeton, 1966). Klaus Schwabe, *Woodrow Wilson, Revolutionary Germany and Peacemaking 1918–1919* (London, 1985) ends the war. Bernard Michel, *La Chute de l'Empire austro-hongrois* (Paris, 1991) recounts the disintegration of Central Europe in absorbing detail.

Chapter 7: see Stanford J. Shaw, *From Empire to Republic: The Turkish War of National Liberation 1918–1923* (5 vols., Türk Tarih Kurumu, 2000) and Michael Llewellyn-Smith, *Ionian Vision* (Michigan, 1999), which is extraordinarily fair-minded as between Greeks and Turks. Margaret MacMillan, *Paris 1919* (New York, 2003) is a splendid survey of peace-making, and Robert Skidelsky, *J. M. Keynes: Hopes Betrayed* (London, 1998) is a brilliant book on the intellectual and moral atmosphere of that generation. For the Middle East, David Fromkin, *A Peace to End All Peace* (London, 2005) has been deservedly a bestseller, but there are two older books that make for thought: Walter Laqueur, *A History of Zionism* (New York, 2003) and Elie Kedourie, *England and the Middle East: The Destruction of the Ottoman Empire*. For the upshot in Germany, Samuel Halperin, *Germany Tried Democracy* (rep. New York, 1965) is a journalist's very well informed account, though it should be read together with H. A. Winkler, *Weimar 1918–1933* (Munich, 1999). On the catastrophe of the inter-war period, the first hundred or so pages of A. J. P. Taylor's *Origins of the Second World War* (London, 1963, with 'second thoughts') sum up the enormous gap between aspiration

and reality. The same conclusion comes, very enter-
tainingly, through Malcolm Muggeridge, *The Thirties*
(written in 1939).

Finally some works of fiction. The generation of 1914
was highly literate, and wrote more and better than that
of 1939. The novels that I should put at the top of my
own list are Louis-Ferdinand Céline, *Voyage au bout de
la nuit*, C. S. Forrester, *The General*, Sebastian Faulks,
Birdsong and, most recent, Louis de Bernieres, *Birds
Without Wings*. The compliment in all cases is that I read
them without stopping.

Index

air war, 126–7, 142, 163–4,
    167, 172
aircraft, 14, 126
Aisne: battle (1918), 168–70;
    stalemate (1914), 46–7
Alexeyev, Genl Mikhail, 87–8
Alsace-Lorraine, British war
    aim, 160
Amiens (1918), 164–5, 171–2
anti-Semitism, 189
Antwerp, 42, 44
Aosta, Emanuel, Duke of, 150
Ardennes, French defeat (1914),
    42
Armenian massacres (1915), 72–3
armistice negotiations (Western
    Allies), 177–81; *see also*
    Brest-Litovsk
arms race, 17–18
Arras, battles (1917 & 1918),
    129, 173

artillery, 38; air support, 142,
    163–4, 167; British, 101–3,
    105, 129, 139, 142, 164,
    175; communications, 102,
    127; counter-battery fire,
    169, 175; creeping barrage,
    105, 118, 127, 139, 141;
    French, 41, 170; German, 41,
    95, 143–4, 148, 163–4, 167,
    169
atomic bomb, 30, 67
Australia: Gallipoli campaign
    (1915–16), 73; Western front
    (1918), 175
Austria, 8–9; alliance with
    Germany, 21, 23, 25–6, 51,
    58–9; arms race, 17; Balkans
    and, 10, 13, 16–17; casualties
    and losses, 59, 80, 108, 145;
    end of empire, 176–7;
    financial situation, 37; treaty

Austria – *cont.*
  of Brest-Litovsk, 5;
  unreliability, 21; war with
  Italy, 82, 97, 144–51; war
  with Russia, 25–6, 26–7,
  50–54, 81, 82, 107–11; war
  with Serbia, 25, 50–54

Badoglio, Genl Pietro, 147
Balkan Wars, 14–15, 16, 21
Balkans, 10, 13, 89, 110–11,
  176, 187
Baltic states, 6, 88, 143–4, 160
Bapaume, battle (1918), 173
Belgium: casualties and losses,
  56; invaded by Germany,
  27–8, 41–2, 42–4; key to
  peace negotiations, 121–2,
  159; territorial ambitions,
  179
Belleau Wood, battle (1918),
  169
Below, Genl Otto von, 146–51,
  162–3
Benedict XV, Pope, 146
Berendt, Brig Richard von, 148
Beseler, Genl Hans von, 88
Bethmann Hollweg, Theobald
  von, 18–19, 24, 26, 30,
  121–3
Bezobrazov, Genl Vladimir M.,
  98, 110

Bismarck, Otto, Prince von, 7,
  9–10, 14, 23, 74
Blitzkrieg (Hutier tactics), 142,
  144, 163; employed by
  British (1918), 171–2;
  employed by French (1918),
  170–1; *see also* Hutier, Genl
  Oskar von
blockade, of Germany, 65–70,
  74, 117, 118–19, 125
Boghos, Nubar, 72
Böhn, Genl Hans von, 169
Bolsheviks, 6, 37, 131–6
Breslau (German battleship), 60
Brest-Litovsk, armistice treaty
  (1918), 5–7, 157–8, 166; *see
  also* armistice negotiations
  (Western Allies)
British army: Arras (1917 &
  1918), 129, 173; British
  Expeditionary Force, 42, 43,
  45, 46–7, 77–9; casualties
  and losses, 56, 73, 103, 105,
  136–7, 162, 164, 168;
  counter-attack (1918),
  171–2, 173–5; Gallipoli
  campaign (1915), 73; and
  German March offensive
  (1918), 160–66; new armies,
  100–1; Somme (1916),
  101–106; trenches, 57;
  Ypres/Passchendaele, 56–7,

76, 128, 136–7, 138–43, 166–7; *see also* Great Britain

Brooke, Rupert, 71, 72

Brusilov, Genl A. A., 106–10

Brusilov offensive (1916), 106–11

Bucharest, 111

Bulgaria, 89, 176

Bülow, Field Marshal Karl von, 45, 46

Byng, Genl Sir Julian, 164

Cadorna, Genl Luigi, 145–6, 147, 150, 166

Cambrai, battle (1917), 142–3, 160

Canadian army, 129, 175

Capello, genl Luigi, 147, 149

Caporetto, battle (1917), 8, 147–51, 160, 165–6, 166

Carpathian campaigns, 53–4, 81–6; *see also* Przemysl

Caucasus: fighting between Turkey and Russia, 60, 70; German oil ambitions, 158

Cavour, Count Camillo, 14

Céline, Louis-Ferdinand, 35

Central Powers: *see* Austria; Germany

Champagne (1915), 79

Chantilly conference (1915), 93, 97, 100

Château Thierry, battle (1918), 169

Chemin des Dames, French attacks (1917 & 1918), 129–30, 131, 171

China, 15, 159

Churchill, Sir Winston S., 8, 27, 59, 66, 120; Dardanelles and Gallipoli, 71–3

Clemenceau, Georges, 131, 185

Conrad von Hötzendorf, Genl Franz Graf, 50–54, 58–9, 75, 80, 83, 97

Constantinople, offered to Russia, 71, 75

Currie, Genl Sir Arthur, 171

Czernin, Count Ottokar, 22

Debeney, Genl Marie-Eugene, 170–71

Diaz, Maj Genl Armando, 151

Douaumont Fort (Verdun), 95, 96

Doughty-Wylie, Lt Col Hotham, 89

Drocourt-Quéant, battle (1918), 173

Duchêne, General Denis Auguste, 168

East Prussia, 44, 47–50

Ebert, Friedrich, 30

Eichhorn, Genl Hermann von,
158
Einstein, Albert, 30
Eisenhower, Genl Dwight D., 13
Entente Cordiale, 13
Enver Pasha, 16, 60, 72–3, 176
Erzberger, Matthias, 179

Falkenhayn, Genl Erich von:
Eastern front, 55, 80–81,
82–3, 86, 88–9; relations
with Conrad, 97; removed
from command of 9th Army,
110; replaces Moltke, 54–5,
59, 74–6; Verdun offensive,
93–7
Falklands Islands, battle (1914),
67
Finland, 6, 158
Foch, Marshal Ferdinand, 45,
166, 171, 181
forts, futility of, 38
France: alliance with Russia,
10; arms race, 17; defence of
Verdun (1916), 93–7;
financial situation, 37;
German ultimatum (1914),
27; mobilization in 1870, 26;
rivalry with Germany, 10;
treaties with Britain and
Russia, 13; *see also* French
army

Franco-Prussian War (1870), 26
Franz Ferdinand, Archduke,
22–3, 25
Franz Joseph, Emperor of
Austria, 111–12, 117
French, Genl Sir John, 43, 45,
79
French army: casualties and
losses, 43, 96, 105, 168;
Champagne (1915), 79;
Chemin des Dames (1917 &
1918), 129–30, 131, 171;
counter-attack (1918),
170–1; methods and
uniforms, 41; mutinies
(1917), 130; response to
German attacks (1914),
41–7; Somme advances
(1916), 103–4; Verdun,
93–7; *see also* France
Friedrich, Archduke, 58

Gallipoli campaign (1915–16),
71–3
Gallwitz, Genl Max von, 87
Georgia, 158
German army: attack in the
west (1914), 41–7; Cambrai
counter-attack, 143;
Caporetto (1917), 146–51,
160; Carpathian campaigns
(1915), 81–6; casualties and

losses, 48, 56, 80, 96, 105, 168, 171, 172, 175; communications problems, 44; defences at Passchendaele (1917), 138–9; in East Prussia, 47–50; Eastern front advances (1915), 84–9; *Friedenssturm* offensive, 170; influence on policy, 20–21, 23–4, 26; March offensive (1918), 8, 160–70; Masurian Lakes winter battle (1915), 81; operation 'Alberich' (1917), 128; retreat (1918), 171–6; Somme (1916), 101, 103–4; 'storm-troops', 143, 144, 163; training and equipment, 40–41; Verdun offensive, 93–7

German navy, 10, 11–13; battleships sent to Turkey, 60; Jutland (1916), 100; submarine warfare, 117, 118–20, 123, 158; suicide plan and mutinies (1918), 180

Germany: alliance with Austria, 21, 23, 25, 50–2, 58–9; alliance with Russia, 10; armistice negotiations (1918), 178–81; armistice with Russia (Brest-Litovsk), 5–7,

157–8; chaos and insurrection, 181; financial situation, 36; Hindenburg Programme, 118, 159, 168; Hitler chancellorship, 189–90; invasion of Austria (1918), 177; naval build up, 10, 11–13; peace negotiations (1917), 121–3; prewar confidence, 7–12; props up Austria at Caporetto (1917), 146–50, 160; response to British blockade, 66–70, 74, 117–18, 118–20; Schlieffen Plan, 20–21, 26–7, 27, 40, 124; 'stab in the back' fantasy, 189; submarine warfare, 117, 118–24; Turkey and, 16, 59–60; war declarations, 24–8; war-economic conditions (1918), 159, 175; Weimar Republic, 187–9

Goeben (German battleship), 60

Gorlice (1915), 166

Gough, Genl Sir Hubert, 140–1, 161–2, 164

Great Britain: allied financier, 93, 126; Belgium and, 27–8; blockade of Germany, 65–70, 125; conscription introduced, 69–70; declares war on

Great Britain – *cont*.
Germany, 28; defensive
alliances, 13, 18; effect of
increased exports, 69;
financial situation, 36–7,
125–6; foreign policy since
1850, 159–60; German envy,
11–12; losses to U-Boats,
123; Middle East territories,
186; munitions industry, 101;
signs of war-weariness, 112;
war with Turkey, 70–4; *see
also* British army; Royal
Navy
Grey, Sir Edward, 36
Guise, 45

Haig, Field Marshal Sir
Douglas, 79, 100–106, 126,
129, 137, 140–42, 162–3,
166–8, 171–2, 175
Hall, Adm Sir William, 125
Hamilton, Genl Sir Ian, 72
Hankey, Maurice, 67
Harrach, Count Franz von, 22
Helfand, Alexander (Parvus),
152
Helfferich, Karl, 121
Hemingway, Ernest, 151, 152
Hindenburg, Genl Paul von,
48–50, 80, 109, 173, 180,
188

Hitler, Adolf, 14, 29, 75, 163,
180, 188–9
Holland, naval blockade and, 68
Holtzendorff, Adm Henning
von, 121, 123, 126
horses, indispensability of and
drawbacks, 38–9, 44, 84
Hötzendorf: *see* Conrad von
Hötzendorf
Hoyos, Count, 24
Hungary, 21–2, 177
Hutier, Genl Oskar von, 160;
see also Blitzkrieg (Hutier
tactics)

India, German threat (1918),
159
industry, war industry, 13–14,
19–20, 101
infantry tactics: advance inline,
102; assault battalions (storm
troops/stosstrupps), 143, 144,
163; fire and movement, 127
influenza epidemic (1919), 186
Iraq: *see* Mesopotamia
Isonzo battles, 136, 144–5
Italy, 8; appeals for Russian
help, 106; Caporetto (1917),
146–51; casualties and losses,
136, 145, 154; colonial
ambitions, 14; Isonzo battles,
136, 144–5; war with

Austria, 81–2, 97, 144–51, 177

Ivanov, Genl Nikolai, 84, 86

Jellicoe, Adm Sir John, 100
Joffre, Marshall Joseph, 42, 45, 118
Joseph Ferdinand, Archduke, 107
Jutland, battle (1916), 100

Karl I, Emperor of Austria, 121
Kemal Atatürk, 60, 73
Khan of Nakhichevan, 39
Kisch, Egon Erwin (journalist), 61
Kitchener, Field Marshal Lord, 45
Kluck, Genl Alexander von, 43–5, 46
Königsberg, 47, 49
Kovno, 87, 88
Kress von Kressenstein, Genl Friedrich, 60
Kriemhild Line, 174, 175
Kühlmann, Richard von, 159
Kuropatkin, Genl Alexei, 98
Kut el Amara, British surrender (1916), 74

Lake Narotch, battle (1916), 98
Lammasch, Heinrich, 177

Lanrezac, Genl Charles, 42
Lawrence, T. E., 186
Le Cateau, battle (1914), 43–4
League of Nations, 186–7
Leinster, RMS, 179
Lemberg (Lvov), 54, 86
Lemke, Mikhail, 98
Lemnos, 72
Lenin, Vladimir I., 30, 134–6, 152, 157, 158
Leopold of Bavaria, Prince, 5
Levetzow, Captain Magnus von (German navy), 180
Libya, 14
Liège, 38, 41, 48
Liman von Sanders, Genl Otto, 16
Lithuania, 7
Lloyd George, David, 28, 117, 129, 136, 160, 181, 185, 189
London, Declaration of (1909), 68
Loos, battle (1915), 77
Lossberg, Col von, 138, 171
Lossow, Genl Otto von, 158
Ludendorff, Genl Erich: Austro-Hungarian army and, 109; defeat, 178–80; East Prussia, Poland and Baltic, 48–50, 80–1, 88; March offensive and retreat (1918), 162–76; master in Germany, 122,

Ludendorff, Genl Erich – *cont.*
158–9, 160; recognises
Western front conditions,
117; relations with Conrad,
58–9; 'stab in the back'
fantasy, 189
Lusitania (RMS), 120
Lvov (Lemberg), 54, 86
Lys, battle (1918), 168

Mackensen, Field Marshal
August von, 83, 87, 89
malaria, 72, 111
Mametz, battle (1916), 103–4
Mangin, Genl Charles, 170
Marne: battle (1914), 45, 45–7;
battle (1918), 170–71
Marwitz, Genl Georg von der,
81, 110, 160
Masurian Lakes, 50; Winter
Battle (1915), 81
Maubeuge, 44
Max of Baden, Prince, 178,
180–81
Mesopotamia, 59; British
Expeditionary Force, 72, 74
Messines Ridge, battle (1917),
137
Metz, 42
Mexico, Zimmerman telegram,
125
Moldavia, 111

Moltke, Genl Helmuth von, 44,
46, 48, 51, 54–5
Monash, Genl Sir John, 171
Mons (1914), 43
Morhange-Sarrebourg, 42
Morocco, Germany and, 13, 14
Mount Kemmel (1918), 167,
173
Mussolini, Benito, 14, 29

Namur, 42, 43, 44
Narotch: *see* Lake Narotch
Naumann, Friedrich, 8–9
Neuve Chapelle, battle (1915),
77
New Zealand, Gallipoli
campaign (1915–16), 73
Nicholas II, Tsar of Russia, 133
Nicholson, Sir Arthur, 18
Nivelle, Genl Robert, 95, 96,
118, 126, 127–30
Novogeorgievsk, 87

oil, importance of, 59, 158,
176, 181
Ottoman Empire: *see* Turkey

Papen, Lt Col Franz von, 74–5
Parvus (Alexander Helfand),
152
Passchendaele, battle (3rd
Ypres, 1917), 137, 138–43,

162; German offensive
(1918), 167–8
peace negotiations (1917),
121–3; *see also* armistice
negotiations (Western Allies);
Brest-Litovsk
peace treaties (1919), 185
Pedroncini, Guy, 130, 152
Pétain, Marshal Henri-Philippe,
95, 130–31, 141, 170
Piave, Italian resistance (1917),
151
Plumer, Genl Herbert, 137, 141
poison gas: British use of, 78,
172; German use of, 76, 143,
148, 164
Poland, 8, 10, 86
Popper, Karl, 30
Porsche, contribution to German
war effort, 146, 151, 165
Porsche, Ferdinand, 8
Portuguese army, Ypres salient
(1918), 167
Potoriek, Genl, 22, 53–4
Princip, Gavrilo, 22–3
Prittwitz, Genl Maximilian von,
48
Przemysl, 58, 59, 79–81, 86; *see
also* Carpathian campaigns

railways: eastern front, 51–3,
84; Gallipoli, 72; strategic

importance, 18–19, 26, 43,
47–8; western front, 43–4,
53, 103, 168
Rastenburg, 50
Rawlinson, Genl Sir Henry,
171
Riezler, Kurt, 24, 29–30, 67,
152
Riga offensive (1917), 143–4,
160
Romania, 81, 110–11
Rommel, Captain (later Genl)
Erwin, 146, 149
Roosevelt, Eleanor, 30
Roosevelt, Franklin D., 30
Royal Navy, 27; blockade,
65–70; counters to U-Boat
threat, 123–4; Dardanelles
disaster (1915), 71; Jutland
(1916), 100
Russia, 10; armistice with
Germany, 5–7, 157–8; arms
race, 17–18; Bolshevik
revolution (1917), 37, 131–6;
Civil War, 186; German
protectorate, 158; inflation
and famine, 134; Ottoman
Empire and, 16; preparations
for war, 17–20; relations
with Germany (1915), 73;
subsidized by Britain, 126;
under Stalin, 187

Russian army: Brusilov offensive (1916), 106–11, 172; Carpathian campaigns, 53–4, 82–6; casualties and losses, 49, 85, 87, 88, 98, 110, 111; collapse and retreat (1915), 86–9, 172; communications problems, 48; exemptions, 57–8; Lake Narotch (1916), 98; Masurian Lakes Winter battle (1915), 81; mobilization and initial moves, 25–6, 27, 47–54; Petrograd mutinies (1917), 131–3; Riga (1917), 143–4; siege of Przemysl (1915), 79–81; transport problems, 58

Russo-Japanese war (1904–5), 26

Rutherford, Sir Ernest, 123

St Gond, French attacks (1914), 45

St Mihiel salient, 94, 174

St Quentin, battle (1918), 173

Salonica, 110–11, 176

Samsonov, Genl Alexander, 48, 49

Sarajevo, 22–3

Schiedemann, Philipp, 179

Schlieffen, Field Marshal Alfred von, 20, 40

Schmoller, Gustav, 120

Schörner, Lt (Later Genl Field Marshal) Ferdinand, 146

Schulenburg, Friedrich Graf von der, 94

Schuster, Sir Felix, 36

Seeckt, Hans von (11th Army Chief of Staff), 86

Serbia, 15, 21; Austria and, 50–54; overwhelmed (1915), 89; in Salonica, 110

Sering, Max, 120

Siegfried Line, 174–5

Smirnov, Genl, 98

Somme, battle of the (1916), 101–6

Stalin, Joseph, 187

Stolypin, Pyotr, 20

submarines, unrestricted warfare, 117, 118–24

Suez Canal, Ottoman attack (1915), 60

Szilard, Leo, 30

Talat Pasha, 60, 72

tanks, 104–5, 127, 142, 170–72

Tannenberg, battle (1914), 49–50

Taylor, A. J. P., 21–2

Teleszky, János, Baron, 37
Teschen, 58
Thionville, 42
Trade Unions, Russia, 133
trench systems and warfare,
    56–7
Trotsky, Leon, 152, 157
Truman, Harry S., 30
Turkey, 10; alliance with
    Germany, 15–16, 59–60;
    Arab provinces, 70, 176;
    Armenians (1915), 72–3;
    armistice (1918), 176;
    casualties and losses, 73; the
    Caucasus and, 60, 70, 176;
    Dardanelles and Gallipoli
    campaign (1915–16), 71–3;
    Holy War declared, 70; loss
    of empire in Africa and
    Balkans, 14–15; Sèvres and
    Lausanne Treaties (1921 &
    1923), 186; warships
    commandeered by Britain,
    59–60

Ukraine, 6, 158
United States of America:
    armistice negotiations (1918),
    179–81; blockade and, 68,
    70, 124; declares war on
    Germany, 123–6; German
    Submarine warfare and,
118–19, 120, 123; von
    Papen's sabotage attempt,
    74–5
United States Army, in France,
    162, 169–70, 171, 173–4,
    175

Verdun, 45, 93–7, 127–8
Versailles Treaty (1919), 185,
    187
Villers-Cotterêts, French
    counter-attack (1918), 170,
    172
Vilna, 88
Vimy Ridge, battle (1917),
    129
Vittorio Veneto, battle (1918),
    177

war: the build up, 7–8, 12–28;
    illusions, 38–9; Napoleonic
    parallels, 65–6
Warsaw, 86
Weber, Max, 11–12, 29, 124
Wells, H. G., 104
Wesendonck, Otto-Günther
    von, 159
Wilhelm II, Kaiser, 9, 25, 51,
    83, 96, 170, 172, 178,
    179–81
Wilhelm (Friedrich Wilhelm),
    Crown Prince, 94, 96

Wilson, Thomas Woodrow, 117, 118, 121–2, 125, 136; Fourteen points, 160, 177, 179; Peace treaties (1919), 185

'Young Turks', 16, 60, 70, 72, 176

Ypres: first battle (1914), 55–6; second battle (1915), 74, 128; third battle (1917), 137, 138–43; German offensive (1918), 167–8

Zeppelins, 120
Zimmermann telegram, 125